WORLD WITHOUT MONEY: COMMUNISM

BY THE FRIENDS OF 4 MILLION YOUNG WORKERS

Print ISBN: 978-0-4229-1506-9

A Radical Reprint

PATTERN
BOOKS

1. What is Communism?

Communism is the negation of capitalism. A movement produced by the development and success of the capitalist mode of production, which will culminate with the destruction of the latter and the birth of a new type of society. Where there currently exists a world based on wage labour and the commodity, there must instead be a world where human activity will never take the form of wage labour and where the products of that activity will not be objects of commerce. Our era is the era of this metamorphosis. It displays the conjuncture of the basic elements of the capitalist crisis and all the requisite means for a communist resolution of this crisis. To describe the principles of communism, to examine how they will ensure the future life of humanity, and to show they are currently unfolding right before our eyes—these are the objectives we shall try to achieve in this text.

Science Fiction?

We would like to depict the world of tomorrow, the communist society we desire. This will not take the form of an attempt to rival science fiction or journalism by presenting a report on the life of the peoples and the animals of the future. We do not have a time machine.

Despite the intriguing nature of the question we cannot predict who will win the war between slacks and skirts, or between the sausages of La Garriga and those of Mallorca. Nor can we even guarantee that humanity will have a future. What makes us so sure that we will not be erased by a nuclear war or a cosmic cataclysm?

Nevertheless, prediction is desirable and possible. We want to describe communist society on the basis of its general regulatory principles. It is necessary to show that tomorrow can be more than just an improved or reformed version of today.

In order not to give the impression of taking too much for granted, we shall go into detail and we shall provide examples. You do not have to take this seriously. You can take it or leave it.

The future is not neutral. Capital has a tendency to occupy and subjugate all social space. But it cannot organize the commerce of its commodities and its wage workers between past and future the way the science fiction authors imagine it will be done. Capital takes revenge for this failing on the field of publicity and ideology. It invites us to live in the future now, to buy the clock or the car or the washing machine of the future. Images of a capitalist future fill our present.

To discuss the communist organization of society, despite the risk of error, is to begin to lift the stone slab that is crushing our lives.

The old question of the reactionaries, "But what do you propose as an alternative?", must be immediately rejected. We are not in the business of selling ideas. We do not have to advertise a society that does away with the market the way one advertises a new brand of soap. Communism is neither an object of commerce nor of politics. It is their radical critique. Communism is not a program that can be submitted to the vote of electors or consumers, not even if it is a democratic vote. It is the hope of the proletarian masses to abandon forever their condition of being mere electors or consumers. Those who put themselves in the position of simple spectators, who believe they can judge without getting involved, are excluded from the debate.

If it is possible to speak of the revolutionary society this is because it is already being born within the society of the present.

Some people will find our propositions insane or naïve. We do not expect to convince everyone. If such a thing were possible, it would be very disturbing. We would rather have readers who have to rub their eyes before granting credence to our positions.

The proletarian revolution will be the victory of simplicity over a servile and sterile science. All of this calls for care around demonstrations. There is a risk that they will take place not in the tranquillity of the laboratory but violently and palpably.

Before saying what communism is, we have to make some things clear right away. It is necessary to denounce the lies surrounding it and to clearly express just what communism is not. Since communism is such a simple reality, so closely linked to everyday life, with which it is identified, the worst counter-truths have not failed to proliferate around communism. This is a paradox only for those who are unaware of the fact that in the "society of the spectacle" it is precisely the meaning of what is quotidian and familiar that must be rejected.

2. Communism or Capitalism?

The prevailing view holds that communism is in principle a doctrine elaborated in the 19th century by the famous Siamese twins named Karl Marx and Frederick Engels, and that this doctrine would be perfected a little later by the founder of the Bolshevik State, Lenin. It would be applied with more or less nastiness in a certain number of countries: the USSR, Eastern Europe, China, Cuba.... In this context people debate whether Yugoslavia or Algeria are socialist, capitalist, or mixed regimes. The reader will forgive us if we do not sing the praises of the benefits of such socialism or communism. We will not confuse apples with oranges, the grey monotony of the countries of the East or the personality cult of China with humanity's radiant future.

The Corkscrews

Communism was not founded by Marx, or by Engels, or by the Pharaoh Ramses II. There might be a brilliant inventor behind the origin of the corkscrew or gunpowder or Valencian paella. There is no such inventor at the origin of communism, nor is there one at the beginning of capitalism, either. Social movements are not the affair of brilliant inventors.

After Marx, Engels synthesized a movement that had become conscious of its existence. They never claimed to have invented either the reality or the word. They wrote little about communist society. They helped the Movement and communist theory to dispel the fog of religion, rationalism and utopianism. They encouraged the proletariat not to rely on the plans of reformers or prophets.

Real revolutionaries do not fetishize the ideas of Marx and Engels. They know that they are the fruit of a particular era and that they have their limitations. Both men underwent development and sometimes clashed. One can find "anything" in the works of Marx. It is necessary to exercise discrimination!

We do not claim to be Marxists. But we deny to those who do claim to be Marxists the right to appropriate and falsify the thought of their heroes.

The proof that great men are powerless in the face of historical movements is provided for us by the shameful way that the work of Marx and Engels was distorted in order to be used against communism.

Some individuals are more gifted and perceptive than the mass of their contemporaries. Class society cultivates these differences. Their impact is felt within the communist movement. We are not talking about whether the leaders or the people make history. We are saying that the work of Marx, like that of Fourier, Bordiga or any other spokesperson for communism, transcends the simple point of view of the individual. Communism does not deny differences in ability, it does not reduce its theoreticians to playing the role of simple amplifiers of the will of the masses but to the contrary is the bitter enemy of careerism, the Führer principal and celebrity worship.

Communism is neither an ideology nor a doctrine. Just as there are communist actions there are also communist words, texts, and a communist theory, but action is not the application of an idea. Theory is not the pre-established battle plan or social blueprint that can be most effectively translated into reality. Communism is not an ideal.

The countries that proclaim their adherence to Marxism-Leninism are not just places where the principles of communism have been misapplied for one reason or another. These countries are capitalist countries. Their regimes display some anomalous characteristics but they are just as capitalist as any liberal regime. It could be argued that a country like Poland or East Germany is much more capitalist than many underdeveloped countries in the "free world". In these countries "communists" are fighting against certain spontaneous tendencies of capital. This is being done for the good of capitalism's general development and is by no means peculiar.

Mandatory planning, collective ownership of the means of production, proletarian ideology ... none of this has anything communist about it. These are aspects of capitalism that have been accentuated in these countries. All the basic characteristics of the system and of the logic of capital accumulation (re-baptized as "socialist accumulation") are ideally suited for such a regime.

The Capitalist Mode of Production

To see socialism or communism in the Marxist-Leninist regimes is to demonstrate a lack of understanding of the reality of these regimes, and above all it demonstrates a lack of understanding of the nature of capitalism.

This shows that one thinks that capitalism is based upon the power of a particular class (the bourgeoisie), private property in the means of production, and the unbridled quest for profit. None of these features are fundamental.

The bourgeoisie is the heir of the old mercantile class. After having spent many years consolidating an important but strictly delimited position within agrarian societies, the commercial bourgeoisie began, over the course of the Middle Ages in Europe, to no longer control just commodities but also the instruments of production. Among the latter was human labour power, which it transformed, via wage labour, into a commodity. This was the origin of capitalism.

The bourgeoisie was in power from the moment that it became the ruling class thanks to the power of the economic and industrial forces it controlled which rendered the old forms of production obsolete. But the bourgeoisie can only submit to the laws of its economy. As the owner of capital, it must obey this force that drags it along, deranges it and sometimes drives it to bankruptcy.

The individual or the separate enterprise has some room for manoeuvre, but neither can swim against the current for very long.

No historical class has ever been able to satisfy all of its whims by using the power it ostensibly wielded. Even the worst tyrants could only remain in power by acknowledging the strict limits of their real sovereignty. It is a mistake to seek to explain social phenomena in terms of power. Such an explanation is even less applicable to the capitalist system than to its predecessors.

The class of those who direct the course of capital has been subject to constant permutations by the action of capital itself. What do the rich merchant of the Middle Ages and the modern CEO have in common? Their motivations and their tastes are different. This divergence is necessary so that they can perform the same function in two different moments of capitalist development. The class of feudal lords was distinguished by tradition and inheritance. This was no longer the case for a bourgeoisie whose fortunes could rise and fall by virtue of business success, marriage connections and bankruptcy.

The relations that unite master and slave, lord and serf, are personal relations. Now, however, instead of being bound to one boss the modern proletarian is bound to the system. The chains that bind him are not those of a personal alliance or a particular contract, but those of a direct need to survive, the dictatorship of his own needs. The proletarian, uprooted from his ancestral land on his lord's manorial domain, and separated from the means of production, has no other choice than to prostitute himself. He is free, marvellously free. He can even, should this arouse his enthusiasm, refuse to sell his labour power and starve to death.

A bourgeois or politician could fail as an

individual. In Russia and China an entire section of the international bourgeois class was left in the lurch. It was replaced by a bureaucracy. This bureaucracy is not a radically different class with respect to its predecessor! A "communist" banker or industrial director bears more of a resemblance to his capitalist enemy than the latter does to his counterpart from only fifty years ago, not to mention the 15th or the 18th centuries.

If capitalism, whether of the western or eastern variety, cannot be explained by the power of the bourgeoisie, it is even less possible to explain communism by the power of the proletariat. The advent of communism means the self-destruction of the proletariat.

Private Property

Private property in the means of production is not a constitutive feature of the capitalist mode of production. It pertains only to the juridical sphere. It subsists in the East in the form of the lands owned by individual peasants. In the West it is being progressively diminished by the encroachments of public ownership.

The State often owns large industrial complexes. Although nationalized, the postal services and the railroads have not lost their capitalist nature. Frederick Engels interpreted this tendency of the State to become the owner of productive forces as a general development that would relegate private capitalism to the museum of antiquities.

The development of modern capitalism is tending increasingly to dissociate private ownership from the management of the productive forces. Not only are the directors of nationalized companies not the owners of the capital they control; even in the big private industries, if they are privately owned, ownership is divided into tiny percentage shares of the total capital. The capitalization requirements of big industry are far larger than any particular personal or family fortune could encompass. These corporations function with the money that is provided to them by a mass of small stockholders and savings account depositors who have practically no power at all over the corporations' operations.

The situation of the countries of the East must be understood in the context of this general developmental trend of capital.

Profit

The capitalist is supposed to be motivated by the quest for the maximum profit. The expression "maximum profit" does not mean much. A business owner can try for one day, or for a week, or even for a whole month, to drive men and machines at full capacity if he was assured of a market for his products. But he would run the risk of regretting his imprudence soon enough for having exhausted his capital. The failure of an attempt of this kind took place in China with "the great leap forward". The scale of the expected profits, and consequently, the volume of dividends for the stockholders and the salaries of the managers, and the rate of economic growth are not arbitrarily decided by omnipotent capitalists.

Making money, that is what motivates the capitalist, whether for personal enrichment or for investment. If he does not make money, whether as a result of negligence, virtue or because it is no longer objectively possible, his business will be eliminated. This is also true for the bureaucrat, in the form of fear of administrative sanctions. As for the rest, neither in the USSR nor in China has it been proclaimed that profit has disappeared; to the contrary, profit is sought for the good of the people, to construct communism. It has become an instrument of economic measurement at the service of the planned economy!

In neither the East nor the West, as Marx

explained, can capitalist development be explained by the profit motive. The truth is quite the contrary. The ideas of profit or land rent do not explain the laws of motion of the system. They are only categories by means of which the ruling classes become aware of economic necessities and take action.

Unlike the humanists of the left who see or pretend to see profit as their great enemy, revolutionaries do not allow themselves to succumb to this illusion. They do not blame the system for being immoral; we are not mired in an attachment to a few unprofitable archaic sectors.

Profit will disappear with the revolution. And without delay! Until that moment arrives it will to some extent play a protective role for the workers. It imposes limits on the tyranny of the owners; it obliges them to be careful with their human material. If it were possible to abolish profit while preserving capital, the average business would be inclined to welcome the return of the concentration camps and society would unravel and collapse into the most absolute barbarism. Nazism was not a historical accident; it was the unleashing of forces that were lurking in the lowest rungs of capital's civilization. Profit fixes some limits on the authoritarianism and on the will to dominate and to destroy that are spawned by an inhuman system.

Blame profit! But then you will also have to blame the whole society in which the life of man has become a commodity.

Wage Labour and Industrialization

The capitalist mode of production is constructed on two solid pillars that distinguish it from all modes of production that preceded it.

The first of these pillars is the system of wage labour. There have already been men who rented their charms, their political loyalty, their military ability and even their labour power to other men. But these activities remained marginal in societies composed of small groups among which money and the commodity did not circulate widely. The development of capitalism meant the real introduction of wage labour in the sphere of production, which it would transform into the general form of exploitation.

The second pillar is industrialization, the transformation of man's relations with nature and with respect to his own activity. Man was no longer content with scratching out a bare subsistence from the soil. With industrialization he would assume the task of systematically transforming nature on a constantly increasing scale. Capitalism is an uninterrupted revolution in the methods of production; it is the progress of "science" and "reason", as opposed to fatalism and obscurantism. It is the movement that succeeds the stagnation of agrarian societies.

Communism is not a return to the past. The end of the system of wage labour does not mean the return to slavery or serfdom. The overcoming of the process of the "conquest of nature" and of industrial organization does not mean a return to the stagnation of the past. Communism will render the aggressive and disorderly nature of the action of capital a thing of the past. Its purpose is not to destroy, to compartmentalize and subjugate, but to act comprehensively to humanize the world, and to make it habitable. It will transcend our current industrial practices so as to reconcile the useful and the pleasant. The lost sense of belonging that once connected the human being with his environment will be rediscovered on a higher level.

Capitalism did not emerge one fine day because people suddenly noticed how efficient it is. Its advent was not a triumph of the intellect; it was imposed on the workforce by way of social convulsions that were often cruel and irrational. It encountered resistance; it would retreat for a while only to seize more ground. It "harvested" its wage labourers from the masses of peasants who had previously been uprooted from their lands and reduced to mendicancy.

The movement of capital has a two-faced aspect. On the one hand it is the development of the human and material forces of production, and consequently use values and useful things. On the other hand it is the development of exchange value. The commodity thus already presents this double character; capital is still a commodity but it is also value that must be constantly enlarged.

For many years capital took the form of the commodity. The merchant could, thanks to his ingenuity and cunning, possess and set in motion a growing mass of products. The moneylender did likewise, but only with respect to money. These primitive forms of capital, however, could not continue indefinitely; value was still parasitic and did not create the means required for its accumulation. Only by the unceasing appropriation and crystallization of value in the means of production as capital did it become capable of real expansion. It is a vampire that feeds on value, i.e., human labour; in order to fulfil its purposes, it must develop machinery and productivity. For capital the latter are only means to an end; for us, in the last analysis, these factors are of the utmost significance. This technological development often assumes unsavoury forms—unemployment, deadly weapons, devastation of nature—but it will permit the revolutionary transformation of human activity and create the preconditions for leaving the barbarous era of class societies behind us.

Communism will not overthrow capital in order to return to the early days of the commodity. Commodity exchange is a link in the chain of progress, but it is link between antagonistic parts. It will disappear without however occasioning a return to barter, that primitive form of exchange. Humanity will no longer be divided into opposed groups and enterprises. It will organize to plan and utilize its common heritage, and to distribute tasks and enjoyments. The logic of the gift (sharing) will replace the logic of exchange.

Money will disappear. It is not a neutral instrument of measurement. It is the commodity in which all other commodities are reflected.

Gold, silver and diamonds will have no other value than the value that derives from their specific usefulness. Following Lenin's suggestion we will be able to reserve gold for the construction of public urinals.

The State and Capitalism

In the so-called "communist" countries money continues to circulate undisturbed. The division by international borders, and within these borders, the division of the economy into separate enterprises, works wonders.

The role played by the State in the economy, a role that is legally founded in the public ownership of enterprises, can be explained by the capitalist nature of these countries.

The State and the commodity are old friends. The merchants wanted society to be unified, so that thieves and robbers could be suppressed and the standard of monetary exchange regulated. With the increasing circulation of goods and people, the State and its bureaucracy discovered the means to become free of the dominant power of the agrarian sector.

The modern State, whether monarchy or republic, is the product of the dissolution of feudal structures by capital. The latter set itself in opposition to particular interests as a representative of the general interest. Capital had to do this because this helped it to overcome those contradictions and oppositions that it could not avoid provoking. The monarchy and the bourgeoisie, despite some momentary friction, stuck together against the feudal powers. Political unification was necessary for the development of commercial and industrial enterprises. Large fortunes and accumulated wealth made the State stronger and more independent. The State often intervened directly to allocate or consolidate the capital necessary for one or another industrial sector. It established the legal arsenal necessary for the development of a supply of free labour. It liquidated the old customs and dissolved ancient bonds. When the bourgeoisie made its appearance on the political stage it had already been a dominant force for many years and the monarchy had long been its servant.

In Russia and Japan, countries that made their appearance on the international stage while still barely industrialized, it was the State that initiated and organized the development of capitalism. It did so in order to preserve the basis of its own power, so as to have a supply of modern weapons. By putting capital at its service it only bowed to the superiority of the latter. The monarchy initiated a process that would end with its own destruction. The necessary preconditions for this grafting operation were not present everywhere. If it was successful in Japan this was because the State was already independent and trade was already highly developed. In China the process at first failed to take hold, and the same was true for most of the other pre-capitalist countries.

The State must often intervene in order to constrain a capital that is acting irresponsibly and to invest more in one place than in another. The bureaucratic regimes only accentuate this tendency towards a never achieved goal.

Does the capitalism of the East create the conditions for a more harmonious or more rational expansion of capital than the capitalism of the West? The question does not make much sense. That such a question can arise is the result of the defects of traditional capitalism. If this traditional capitalism is now re-imported to Moscow or Leningrad it is because of the defects of the capitalism of the East.

Wherever the bourgeoisie remained in a state of underdevelopment due to the economy, the bureaucracy conquered political power by relying on the support of certain social forces like the proletariat or the peasantry. But this could not reduce the impact of the disintegrating effects of international capitalism on traditional society. The bureaucracy had no other choice; it could not, as it wished, establish traditional capitalism and make it fertile; this was because of its social base of support and its lack of capital. Learning from experience it found a way that conformed with its nature and which allowed it, at the expense of the peasantry, to accumulate industrial capital.

The bureaucracy is a unifying force that has facilitated the authoritarian transfer of wealth from one sector of society to another. It modifies the spontaneous development of capital in favour of its goal of retaining power. But capital is not a neutral force that can be used for any purpose whatsoever. The bureaucracy plans, it rules. But what does it plan, what does it rule over? The accumulation of capital. It restricts the free market, it fights against the black market that is constantly re-emerging; but this is not the proof of its anti-capitalism but only a sign that the essential basis of capital is still alive and well.

The western States themselves have been led to intervene even more directly in the play of the economic forces. They must have a social policy and they must undertake planning. Bureaucratization is not a phenomenon restricted to the East. It affects the democratic and the fascist States as well as the big private corporations. It is the product of and the bleak remedy for the increasing atomization of society.

In a certain sense it is incorrect to speak of the bureaucratic capitalism or State capitalism of the countries of the East. All modern capitalist forms are bureaucratic and statist.

State ownership of all industry does not, however, signify absolute control; legal power is not the same thing as real power.

In liberal capitalism, the State, relying on the support of popular, military or even bourgeois forces, can confront this or that major corporation; it has the power. This does not, however, allow it to rise above economic laws. It can stand up to the power of the monopolies, but it cannot return to the world of small businesses of the past.

In the capitalism of the East, the bureaucratic State, regardless of the location of its headquarters, cannot abolish commercial categories and competition between enterprises. As long as separate enterprises exist there will be competition even if prices are subject to regulation.

This lack of unity is not limited to the economic sphere. The bureaucracy itself is incessantly rent by factional struggles and conflicts between individuals. Due to a lack of real unity it is the image of unity that must be maintained. The enemy is not a party colleague, but anti-party.

What the bureaucracy gains with regard to economic efficiency, is immediately lost again. The lie and the loss of reality totally suffuse the social body. The silent struggle behind the scenes replaces open competition.

Although it was capable of initiating a burst of economic development in unfavourable conditions, the bureaucracy always trailed behind the technological level attained by the liberal capitalist societies.

Recuperation

Why would capitalists try to pass themselves off as communists? As a general rule capitalists do not like being called capitalists!

The origin of the capitalist claim to the name of communist can be precisely dated to the Russian revolution. The word communist conveys more of the sense that one would bend over backwards for the working class rather than that one recognizes the fact of exploitation. It can give inhuman development of the system a human face: the construction of communism. Or else the masses are presented with some projects called "the new frontier" or the "new society"!

When capital claims to be communist, when it recuperates the thought of Marx in order to denature it in its universities of intellectuals or in order to facilitate the brutalization of the workers in factories, it is only imitating a movement that was completely fulfilled elsewhere. Capital does not create, it recuperates; it feeds on the passion and the initiative of the proletarians, which is to say: it feeds on communism.

You will not be able to understand much about communism if you do not understand the capitalist nature of the countries of the Eastern Bloc. The revolutionary battles of its past must not be allowed to rehabilitate Stalinism, since it is a fundamentally anti-communist system and ideology. The fact that bastions of the working class still exist within its domains must not cause us to become indulgent, but to the contrary, it must incite us to refuse any compromise with it.

One does a great service to Stalinism by not criticizing it as a capitalist system. Some revolutionaries, anarchists in particular, have recognized Stalinism as communism so as to be able to associate the latter term with authoritarianism. Authority—that is the monster! Under the guise of analysis the search for the origin of this authoritarianism goes all the way back to the personality of Karl Marx.

The Trotskyists, following in the footsteps of their leader, the unfortunate enemy of Stalin, have manufactured explanations as elaborate as they are silly. Socialist base and capitalist superstructure coexist, at least, in the USSR; as for the other countries, the jury is still out. In any event, they never understood anything about communism; no more than Trotsky, who thought compulsory labour was a communist principle. They are not revolutionaries; Trotsky was, but he was never anything but a bourgeois revolutionary and then a reluctant bureaucrat. We shall leave this clique with its intellectualism, its Byzantine disputes and its ridiculous organizational fetishism.

The Maoists, those "Stalinist-mystics", reduce the entire problem to a question of politics and morality. The USSR has become social-imperialist and maybe even capitalist. Fortunately, China and Albania, under the wise proletarian leadership of Mao, Enver Hoxha and Bibi Fricotin, have not been contaminated. Communism is profit and politics put at the service of the people!

As communist ideas spread, even in the USSR and China, to satisfy the needs of a proletariat that will become revolutionary, these sects will become increasingly more incomprehensible! They are trying to keep the process of the revolution on the terrain of politics. They are in the vanguard, it is true, but it is the vanguard of capital; in a revolutionary period all the political puppets will try to assume revolutionary airs so as not to be cast aside. It has become something of a tradition for the revolution to be combated in the name of the revolution. The Stalinist or leftist militants who have gone astray will be incorporated into the real party of communism.

Some, not so blind, have acknowledged the fact that society in the capitalism of the Eastern Bloc is divided into social classes. Unfortunately, they have also thought that this capitalism represents a new and superior mode of production. This is doing too much honour to Stalin and his cohorts.

Primitive Society

We see nothing communist about the regimes that claim to be communist. On the other hand, we see communism where it is usually not discerned. Primitive societies that, rejected by "civilization", subsist in arid or inaccessible corners of the earth are communist, although their members live from hunting and gathering or from rudimentary agriculture. This is why we can say that the USSR is not communist but the United States of America was communist several centuries ago!

We do not expect to make humanity return to this stage. Such a project would in any case be very difficult because such a condition requires a very low population density. It is important, however, to rehabilitate primitive and prehistoric humanity.

The Indian was happier and, in a certain sense, more civilized, than the modern American citizen. The cave man did not die of hunger. It is in today's world where hundreds of millions of humans have an empty stomach. Primitive man, as Marshall Sahlins has demonstrated, lived in a state of abundance; he was wealthy, not because he accumulated wealth, but because he lived as he wished. The western traveller who was sometimes paradoxically impressed by his good health before giving him smallpox pities his seeming poverty and his nakedness. Primitive man possessed practically nothing; but for those who live from hunting and gathering this is no disadvantage. His lack of possessions allowed him to move about freely and take advantage of the bounty of nature. His security was not maintained by savings but by his knowledge and his ability to use what his environment provided. He spent less time than a civilized man in earning his livelihood. His "productive" activity had nothing to do with the boredom that characterizes the office or the factory. Fortunate are the Yir-Yiron of Australia, who have the same word for 'work' and for 'play'!

There is a profound difference between the communism of the past and the communism of the future. The former is a society that uses its environment by knowing how to adapt to it, while the latter is a society based on the continuous and profound transformation of that same environment. Between these two communist societies, the period of class societies will appear to be, when viewed in this perspective, a painful but relatively short stage of human history. A small consolation for those who are still immersed in it!

Marx and Engels

Marx and Engels tried to acquire an understanding of the development of capitalist society. They did not spend much time describing the future world that monopolized the attention of the utopian socialists. But one cannot not draw a hard and fast line between the critique of capitalism and the affirmation of communism. The correct understanding of the historical role of money or of the State can only be attained from the point of view of their disappearance.

If Marx and Engels did not have more to say about communist society this is undoubtedly, and paradoxically, not only because this society was not as easily comprehended due to the fact that it was so distant, but also because it was all the more present in the spirits of the revolutionaries of that time. When they spoke of the abolition of wage labour in *The Communist Manifesto* they were understood by those in whom these words found an echo. Today it is more difficult to envisage a world without the State and without the commodity since both have become ubiquitous. But by becoming so ubiquitous they have also lost their historical necessity. Theoretical effort must take over from spontaneous consciousness, before it renders itself superfluous by virtue of the fact that its conclusions have become simple banalities.

Marx and Engels may not have understood the nature of communism as well as Fourier, in the sense of its liberation and harmonization of the emotions. On the other hand, Fourier did not fully reject the wages system insofar as he envisioned, among other things, that doctors should not be paid for treating the illnesses of their patients but rather in accordance with the general state of health of the community.

Marx and Engels nonetheless expressed themselves clearly enough so that they cannot be held responsible for the bureaucracy and the financial policies of the "communist" countries. According to Marx, money disappears immediately with the advent of communism and the producers no longer exchange their products. Engels spoke of the disappearance of commodity production with the advent of socialism. In order to clarify the fact that these statements were not youthful errors, as is so often claimed by the Marxological rabble, we shall draw upon the "Critique of the Gotha Program" and *Anti-Dühring*.

Stalinists of every stripe will speak of the dross in the works of the masters. They will perform a song and dance that proves they are Marxists rather than dogmatists. According to them, money, capital and the State have shed their bourgeois character in order to become proletarian. The boldest will even say that once communism is constructed it might be possible to leave such trinkets behind. According to others communism will be simply a society in which the standard of living will be very, very high. In any event, communism, lost in heaven and the stairway that leads to it, is composed of a multitude of additional modules that form so many transitional stages.

It is true that communism is being constructed in the Eastern Bloc, but its construction is neither better nor more conscientiously undertaken there than it is anywhere else. A revolution will be required for it to be exposed.

The concept of building communism by means of

economic and social instrumentalities is a typically bourgeois idea. Communism is represented in the same way as the production of a manufactured object. Society is seen as an immense factory; it is thought that the whole functions just like the part. Therefore it is a question of will, of planning, of the correct political line....

The error into which these Stalinists fall with respect to the road to follow affects the result. It is no longer a question of making the private enterprise economy disappear, but of transforming the economy into one big enterprise. The conundrum represented by the existence of a police force will disappear; the augmentation of the moral sense by "communist" education will be enough to cause theft and subversion to disappear!

The best solution is of course the one proposed by Joseph Stalin himself. When we cannot change reality, we will change the words. The little father of the people tells us: you want the employees to receive a wage and, through the agency of the State, they are the owners of the enterprises that hire them. You cannot be your own employee! So the wages system is abolished in the Soviet Union. If you are under the impression that you receive a wage, if you are afraid of being fired from your job, this is because you are delusional. Fortunately, our socialist fatherland possesses re-education centres and psychiatric hospitals!

Stalin admitted that commodity production and the division of the economy into separate enterprises still existed, but this was not capitalism because in capitalism the means of production are the property of individuals. Everything boils down, in practice, to questions concerning the legal definition of terms. It is enough for a State to proclaim that it is communist for it to be so.

Since Stalin explained all of this in *The Economic Problems of Socialism in the USSR*, those who have studied this question have had nothing new to contribute to our understanding of the issue.

One can see Mao Tse Tung or Fidel Castro as brave guerrillas and capable politicians. One could maintain that the Chinese suffer less hunger than the Indians and have fewer political freedoms than the Japanese. But regardless of these details, it is still just capitalism.

3. The End of Property

Communism is the end of property. Everyone knows this and it arouses a great deal of discomfort; some of it totally justified. The owners of large estates, of numerous sumptuous homes ... will be obliged to moderate their lifestyle. Industrial and commercial fortunes will disappear. Those who will be expropriated, although today they possess a large part of society's wealth, are a small and well-defined caste. On the other hand, we shall not as a general rule attack individuals; we shall act with reference to the nature of the goods in question. We shall seize the castles but will leave the houses alone, whether they belong to the poor or the rich! The concerns that have penetrated the consciousness of the proletarians and, above all, that of the peasants, are not justified. Communism is not the seizure from the oppressed of the little they possess.

What Is Property?

This question is not so easy to answer. For proof of this, we call the reader's attention to the polemic that pitted Marx against Proudhon. The latter had asserted, "property is theft". Proudhon understood quite well that the origin of property was not nature, but that it was the product of a society in which relations of force, violence and the appropriation of the labour of others prevailed. But if one says that property is theft, and since theft can only be defined in relation to property, we find ourselves in a vicious circle.

The problem only becomes more complicated when one proceeds from the question of property to the question of its abolition. Is it necessary to abolish all property, whether in the means of production or personal possessions? Is it necessary to act selectively? Should we replace private property with collective or State property? Or is it a matter of the radical abolition of all property?

Communism opts for the latter proposal. It is not about the transfer of titles of ownership, but precisely the disappearance of property, plain and simple. In the revolutionary society you will not be able to "use and abuse" something just because you own it. There will be no exceptions to this rule. A building, a pin, a parcel of land: none of these things will belong to anyone, or, if you prefer, they will belong to everyone. The very idea of property will soon be considered to be an absurdity.

In that case, will everything belong equally to everybody? Will the first person who comes along be able to evict me from my house, strip me of my clothing, and take the bread from my mouth because I no longer own my house, or my clothing, or my food? Of course not; the material and personal security of each person will, to the contrary, be reinforced. Simply stated, it will no longer be the right of ownership that will be invoked for protection but the interest of the person in question will be the direct criterion. Each person must be able to feed himself in proportion to his hunger and seek lodgings and clothing at his convenience. Each person must be able to enjoy peace of mind. Certain ideologues want to see property as merely the extension of the animal's territoriality into human society; in this way property would no longer be a fact pertaining to a specific era or even of a specific species, but as belonging to all animals. However, no one has ever seen a fox or a bear rent the territory that he owns, or inhabit a territory where he is only a tenant! Such things are nonetheless frequent in our society. It is precisely property which permits the use and the possession of something to be dissociated.

The fact that a good is not property provides no indication regarding the use to which it will be put; all that is certain is that it will be put to some use. A bicycle will be used to travel, and not only so that Mr. Martin, its legitimate owner, may travel. The question regarding whether or not human beings, for sentimental or personal reasons, need a fixed territory and objects with which they identify is not a question that can be answered with reference to the concept of property. So, the dental hygienists can rest assured: we are not proposing to make toothbrushes into common property.

To oppose individualism to collectivism, personal use to social use, in order to make this opposition the crux of a "choice between forms of society" is bourgeois cretinism. From this perspective it would be absolutely necessary to support rail transport against the personal automobile; in this way the communists would be in favour of the collective orgy and the bourgeois would be in favour of masturbation! We laugh at these kinds of disputes, they make no sense outside the context of practical circumstances. What is clear, however, is that we are not the ones who are responsible for the depersonalization and atomization of our existence.

Under current conditions the rights of property constitute a barrier against the destruction of personal life. It is in every possible way a derisory guarantee. It does not stop noise from penetrating the walls of poorly insulated apartments, it is of little avail against eviction; the peasant might be the owner of his land, but his title deed poses no obstacle to the advancing depopulation of the countryside.

Today there are fallow fields, uninhabited houses, wealth of every kind lies unused, and all of this is accepted as necessary; unfortunately the owners do not want, or, what is worse, are incapable, of either using or giving away these goods.

The idea of ownership does have some relationship to reality; it is also, however, a mystification: one can own something without having any power of control over it. It is a double lie: social and economic; and it also affects the relations between man and nature.

Property rights are necessary in capitalism. Exchange requires that everything be clearly defined. When it is a question of business dealings it is necessary to know who really owns a particular commodity and who does not. In the past, local custom could provide a framework for deciding how to use things and arrange matters; but when things acquired a degree of independence from men and could pass from hand to hand, custom was no longer enough. Only faint traces of it remain in the countryside: easement rights, the right to access springs and other sources of water, the right to glean after the harvest.... The commodity and capital need a discreet body of rules that are applicable regardless of the particular circumstances.

In the Middle Ages landed property in the modern sense did not exist. With regard to any particular parcel of land, the rights of the serfs, the local lord, the king, and the church could be exercised.... Until the 19th century a certain number of rules continued to restrict the power of the landowner by restricting him to taking no more than the harvest of the first mowing of a meadow, forbidding him from fencing off his land, forcing him to allow gleaning rights and pasturage of animals on fallow land.

In the world of bourgeois equality everybody is a free proprietor. The peasant owns his land, the industrialist owns his factory and the worker owns his labour power. There is no theft, but there are people who become wealthy and accumulate riches completely out of proportion to what their own labour would make possible. Property conceals relations of exploitation.

If the peasant has become an agricultural landowner and possesses the parcel of land he cultivates, he is no less subject to certain price fluctuations that are completely outside his power. Working constantly, he is nonetheless unable to become rich.

Property does not explain the power of the capitalist enterprise. The enterprise is the owner of fixed capital: buildings, machines, etc. But this does not take into account the wealth that passes through its owner's hands and which constitutes his turnover.

The complex interconnections of the economy

lead to a restriction of the rights of property. What you do in your house can have a negative impact on your neighbour. You cannot throw your wastes in a river with impunity just because you own part of the shoreline.

The absolute character of the right of property— it is "sacred and inviolable" according to the Declaration of the Rights of Man—is insignificant in relation to the forces and the unpredictable events of nature. The most intransigent landowner will be powerless if an erupting volcano were to bury his land; he can call the police, but he will not be able to evict the intruder. As a general rule, natural objects and phenomena do not punctually obey us.

As the nephew of the great chief Cochise noted, the white men spend their whole lives fighting over land. It is not men, however, who can possess the land, but, to the contrary, it is the land that possesses and feeds men. We all end up buried in it sooner or later.

The Agrarian Question

The agrarian question is intimately linked to the solution of the problem of property. It is a vital question for the revolution. In the past, peasant armies suppressed the workers' insurrections. The opposite also took place, as in Mexico. The small peasant has always been easily mobilized by the counterrevolution in the name of the defence of his sacred right to property.

In the industrialized countries, capital has done what it has accused the "reds" of wanting to do. It has expelled the majority of the peasants from their land. It can therefore no longer rely on the frightened masses of peasants to form the ranks of the counterrevolutionary armies. The supply of subsistence goods to the cities is still provided by the countryside, however. The party of order will always be happy to use this situation as a weapon against the revolution.

Where the agricultural workers do not own the land they cultivate, but are tenant farmers or wage labourers working for large estates, they will organize to carry on production. They will not have to answer to their old landlord or boss: the land will go to those who work it! If their former landlord or boss wants to join them in order to contribute his knowledge and labour, this would be of some help, but he will only be able to do so on the basis of equality.

Where ownership and cultivation of the soil coincide, where the peasant employs few or no wage labourers, the problem must be apprehended in a different manner: we must take into account, on the one hand, the interest of society as a whole, which cannot be supplied with food by discontented farmers; on the other hand, we must also take into account the proletarianized peasant, who depends on the capitalist system for his inputs and markets and who should understand that he has everything to gain from the communist revolution.

Capitalist development has taken place at the expense of agriculture. It has absorbed manpower and resources for industry. Communism will reverse this trend. Agriculture is its particular concern because of its role in food production as well as environmental protection. These are two areas where capitalism has demonstrated a distinct lack of prudence.

The institution of property, whether or not it is based on the family, will disappear along with the State and the legal system that legitimizes it. The use and habit of cultivating a particular parcel of land will continue and will even be organized by the revolutionary authorities. The peasants may organize upon this basis or, if they prefer, they may continue to occupy their parcel in isolation. It is likely that, at least for a certain period, both methods will be combined, each peasant being ensconced on his parcel but practicing more mutual aid than is presently the case for certain kinds of work and for the shipment of their products. Inheritance in the strict sense of the word will disappear—but who is more likely to possess the qualifications and the interest to succeed a farmer than his son!

The general rule will be to allow the peasants to organize agricultural production as they see fit. Coercion would be the worst and the most expensive solution of all.

The agricultural collectivization implemented by East Bloc capitalism has nothing to do with communism. It was not for ideological but for economic and class reasons that these programs were put into effect. It was necessary to combat the resurgence of the bourgeoisie in the countryside. The rich peasants were getting rich at the expense of the poor peasants by lending money at usurious rates of interest. They thus created a pole of accumulation for this interest capital that competed with the industrial pole of accumulation upon which the bureaucracy was based. This is why it was necessary to impose and to pay the price of agricultural collectivization.

And a heavy price was paid. In the early stages of collectivization in the Soviet Union, peasant resistance was so strong that the sharecroppers sector was decimated. The long-term consequence was the stagnation of agricultural productivity due to the lack of incentive on the part of the members of the Kolkhozes. This led to frequent policy changes with regard to family-owned farm parcels. Collectivization helped keep the peasants in the countryside by insulating them from the effects of direct economic pressure. This resulted in lower pressure and less competition in the labour market. The USSR preserved an exceptionally large number of peasants considering its level of industrial development. These peasants were dragged in the wake of industrial development like a prison chain gang.

By rejecting collectivization, do we therefore reject the task of revolutionizing and communizing the countryside? Absolutely not! To the contrary! The communist revolution is the liquidation of the commodity economy. This also holds true for the countryside.

The farmer will not make money in exchange for his labours if he is a wage labourer, nor from his commodities if he is an independent producer. He will gratuitously deliver his surplus production to society; in compensation, he will not have to pay for the goods required for his personal needs or his farm operations. He will no longer be motivated by the desire or the need for money. His motivation will be directly rooted in his interest in the work, by his love for his chosen way of life or by the desire to be useful.

The peasant will not have to work as hard as before. He will be able to request assistance from labour power made available by society. This will be made possible by the closure of a plethora of more or less parasitic enterprises and a reduction in the labour power utilized for the purposes of industry and the tertiary sector. It will be possible to provisionally shut down some productive enterprises in the era of giant agriculture in order to free up labour power. This would be unimaginable today.

Distribution, as well as production, will be transformed. The road that leads from the farmer to the consumer will be shortened by as much as possible. Products will be transported directly from a particular agricultural region to a particular city and this process will be organized by those directly involved. When one considers the difference between the price of production and the price paid by the consumer one will understand the significance of such a process of simplification.

The peasants will conduct the labour of cultivation and raising livestock either alone or with assistance from others. They will not work in isolation from the rest of society. We do not promise them absolute freedom. Agriculture depends today, and will continue to depend in the future, on other sectors of the economy. The most prominent such sectors are those that provide fertilizers and agricultural equipment; the independence of the peasants is thus necessarily restricted as a result of this condition. Furthermore, agriculture plays such an essential role that all those who depend on it cannot afford to ignore it.

Let us imagine an extreme case: if some farmers allow land to go uncultivated and herds to go untended because they no longer need to make money, it would be naïve to think that some people will quietly accept their fate and die of hunger. In such a situation it would be possible to cut off supplies to the lazy farmers as a countermeasure. The farmers are responsible for conserving their farmlands and must be able to live a comfortable life, but they must not be allowed to become parasites and, above all, they must not be allowed to hoard certain goods that others could use immediately.

Overcoming the separation of town and countryside is one of the goals of the revolution. This can only be accomplished very slowly since this separation is inscribed in stone and concrete. One cannot wave a magic wand and move skyscrapers here and forests there. It will be possible, however, to rapidly implement measures that will lead in this direction. For example, the provisional or permanent resettlement of urban populations in the countryside where small industrial centres can be established to complement the new population centres and, where this is possible, as adjuncts to local agricultural activities. Many people who were forced to leave the countryside or who find city life unsuitable will be happy to return to the country. Individual and collective gardens will multiply and will beautify these rural settlements and even the urban centres. This will be facilitated by tearing up the pavement of streets that will no longer be necessary due to reduced traffic. This will make it easier to recycle household wastes, reduce transport expenses and provide fresh vegetables to the population. One of the defects of capitalist agriculture is that it has become so separated from the consumer and the latter's wastes and has had to compensate for these deficiencies by means of chemical or biological inputs that have to be constantly increased. In these gardens, children, the elderly and the handicapped who are today refused a role in production and are often destined to lives of boredom, can have something to do and make themselves useful. This will be a magnificent terrain for teaching a deschooled young generation. Finally, this will help clean up our polluted air!

From Scarcity to Abundance

The legal right and the mental attachment to property will die out in communist society because scarcity will become a thing of the past. It will no longer be necessary to hold on tightly to an object in fear of never being able to enjoy it if you turn your back on it for even a single instant.

What kind of magic do you intend to use in order to give birth to this fabulous era of abundance? This is the question that will be sarcastically asked by the bourgeois. There is nothing magical about it: we can make abundance arise because it is already here right in front of our noses. Nothing needs to be done to give birth to abundance except to free it from its bonds. It is capital which, by squeezing humanity and nature for the last two or three centuries, has made abundance possible: it is not communism which, all of a sudden, will produce abundance, but capitalism which has artificially maintained scarcity.

The formidable increase in the productivity of labour has not, or not yet at any rate, changed much with regard to the fate of the proletariat; it has even had negative effects. The power of capital has destroyed the traditional societies of the Third World without allowing its population access to the industrialized world. This factor, together with an enormous demographic expansion has plunged a large part of humanity into profound misery. Under these conditions, wage slavery is a veritable improvement compared to living as a beggar or a pauper.

The impact of nuclear energy and electronics has so far been experienced with respect to their military uses. Scientific progress has fortunately delivered us from those barbarous times when one had to see those one killed and sometimes was even splashed with their blood. Disgusting!!!

Even those inhabitants of the "rich" countries who have benefited from this increase in productivity are exploited. Wage increases and the progressive growth of consumption hardly compensate for the deterioration of their living conditions. Having more or better objects than were available in a previous era does not mean that one lives better. The worker has the car his father did not have, but his workplace and the countryside that he visits on weekends have become more distant. He loses in traffic jams the time he won with the shortening of the working day, and he has traded his physical for nervous exhaustion. With regard to its conditions of development, what industrialization gives with one hand it takes back with the other. It boasts of its remedies but it omits to mention that it was the origin of the illness in the first place. Nor is this accidental: the logic of commodity production requires that conditions of dissatisfaction be maintained. The doctor needs illness. As Fourier pointed out: in civilization scarcity is born from abundance and society moves in a vicious circle.

The human being has been gradually reduced to the passive role of consumer. His moribund state is reanimated with the artificial life of commodities. His misery becomes the technicolour reflection of commodities displayed in all the store windows and on sale for low prices.

In communist society goods will be freely available and free of charge. Social organization will be thoroughly disencumbered of money.

How would it be possible to prevent some people from hoarding wealth to the detriment of others? After a period of euphoria during which we will help ourselves to the existing stock of goods, won't our society risk collapsing into chaos and inequality before totally succumbing to disorder and terror?

These concerns are not restricted to a small

handful of privileged elements with a direct interest in maintaining the present system; they also express the point of view of those among the oppressed who are paralyzed by the fear that a social upheaval will make their situation worse. In the storm the big fish will be better armed for killing the little fish!

In the fully developed communist society the productive forces will be sufficient to provide for all needs. The feverish and neurotic desire to consume and to hoard will disappear. It will be absurd to want to accumulate goods: there will no longer be any money to pocket or wage workers to hire. Why accumulate cans of beans or false teeth that you will never use? In this stage of society, if some form of imposition still exists it will not be a restriction on the distribution of products but rather on the nature of the products, in the conditions that are imposed by the various specific use values of the products; there will necessarily be a selection of some possibilities and a rejection of others at the level of their manufacture.

When revolutionary society has first emerged from the fetters of the old world, the situation will be different. The revolutionary authorities, the workers' councils, will have to formulate and guarantee the observation of a certain number of rules to prevent the resurgence of the habits and procedures of commodity society. Perhaps it will then be necessary to limit the number of cans of beans or pounds of sugar each person may possess in his home. It is not possible to predict just how long this stage will last; it will vary according to the greater or lesser poverty of the regions in question and will depend on the power and the resolve of the revolutionary party. A war provoked by the party of capital, which would cause setbacks for production and transport, would only prolong this transitional phase. If we base our estimate solely on the time required for the communist reconversion of the productive forces, the transitional period could be very brief; we saw how quickly the American economy was able to be transformed into a war economy during the Second World War!

With communism, the nature of production as a whole and the nature of the objects produced will undergo a radical transformation. The disappearance of exchange value will have a major impact on use value.

The Transformation of Products

The commodities offered for sale on the market comprise an extremely hierarchical set of objects. There are not just one or even several commodities for each particular need; there is a multitude of commodities from the same enterprise or from the competition. Of course, this is all about satisfying the public and responding to the variety of its needs. The customer must have a choice! In practice his choice is restricted by his financial means and his social function. Numerous commodities respond to the same need but each one is distinguished by its quality and price; this is true of cookware, for instance. On the other hand, different products correspond to different uses; but these different uses are not available to the same individuals. For example, some people conduct their affairs by means of supersonic jets and other people by means of bicycles.

This hierarchy and differentiation of commodities is the reflection of competition between groups, extreme wage inequality, and the living conditions of the capitalist world. It leaves its mark on industrial development. The needs of the rich play the role of bellwether. Goods like the automobile lose a large part of their quality as articles of use when they cease to be the privilege of a minority and come within the reach of just anybody.

Communism does not propose to make everyone wear the same uniform and eat the same soup; but it will put an end to this disastrous diversification and hierarchy of products. New goods that are still scarce will be put to use first for collective purposes or else on a first-come, first-served basis.

With regard to clothing we can imagine that a reduced number of high quality articles of clothing will be produced, but in sufficient quantity to provide for all sizes and customary uses. They will be produced on a massive scale and by means of as much automation and machinery as possible. At the margins, workshops can be opened where machines and fabrics will be available for those who want to make different clothes for themselves or their friends.

4. Beyond Work

Capitalism has continuously revolutionized the means of production but it has been incapable of really liberating and transforming productive activity. Industrial labour signifies the most extreme form of alienation. The proletarian in blue overalls or white shirt is chained to his machine or to his work routine. He has lost the freedom to give his labour a personal touch or to carry it out in his own way that was the prerogative of the artisan or even the slave and the serf. The impersonal character of this contemporary form of domination makes it unendurable.

Work has been separated from the rest of life. Life is dominated by the fatigue and the brutalization that it engenders and by the wage that it provides.

With the control exercised by modern capital over social life in its entirety, our whole existence has ended up monopolized by the principles of work. The logic of efficiency and productivity dominate our "free" time. Everything must be rational and profitable, including pleasure and "affairs"! Everyone is cordially invited to take over from the system by transforming it.

Communism is first and foremost a radical transformation of human activity. In this respect one can speak of the abolition of work.

Work and Torture

If there is a word that is safely neutral it certainly is not the word for work.

In French and Spanish one of the words for "work" or "labour" (in Spanish, "trabajo", in French, "travail", and with a slightly modified meaning, the English "travail") originated from the Latin word, "trepalium", which denotes an instrument of torture similar to the "rack". Before assuming its modern meaning, this word designated mine labour and then certain kinds of especially hard work. Today its meaning has been considerably extended but its boundaries are still unclear. There is a constant tendency to provide it with a natural justification, however.

In English the word originated in a particular form of activity of the peasant. What characterizes the word for work or labour is precisely its abstract quality. It no longer designates this or that special activity but activity and effort as such. One no longer plants cabbages, or weaves, or herds cattle; one works. All work is basically the same. What counts is the time spent working and the wage earned. As Marx said: "Time is everything, and man is nothing; at most he is the carcass of time."

It is not the word for work that has such an impact as the hateful reality that it represents. It does not even matter if the word disappears. If the word survives it will have to undergo a profound change of meaning. Maybe it will end up as a synonym for the greatest of pleasures!

In communist society productive activity will lose its strictly productive character. The obsession regarding efficiency and punctuality will disappear. Labour will be based on a life transformed in its entirety.

Such a change implies the end of hierarchy, of

the division between order-givers and order-takers, of the separation of decision and execution, of the opposition between mental and manual labour. Man will no longer be ruled by the products of his activity and by his tools. The subjugation of nature to the productive process and its monopolization by groups or individuals will come to an end.

This revolution will be accompanied by a technological transformation. The very nature of industrial development will be called into question.

The parasitic nature of capitalism is expressed in the fact that it is possible to provide a secure foundation for social life even when most businesses are closed. A test regarding the resources contained by a highly developed country was provided by the strike of May 1968 in France. All industry can be shut down for a whole month without any significant consequences for social life.

Maybe there will be a shortage of bread in a revolutionary period. But this shortage cannot be attributed to a lack of productive capacity. It would be due to special causes. This will not prevent us from closing parasitic industries. To the contrary, it would be all the more necessary in order to be able to redirect existing resources towards vital sectors.

One cannot say in advance and in detail what will be eliminated and what will be retained. We are convinced of the despicable role played by war industries. They will have no reason to exist once communist society has been fully established. In the meantime one cannot rule out its further development in communism's early stages!

Such decisions, in all cases, will not be taken by a committee of technocrats but directly by the workers affected by the decisions. The threat of a loss of wages will no longer play a role in their deliberations!

If some workers, due to corporativism or for less respectable reasons, cling to useless or even harmful enterprises, they will have to answer to the entire communist proletariat. The right to property or self-determination will be no excuse for police or financial workers to seek to perpetuate the routine of their usual work!

Everything that serves finance and the state machine will be eliminated or at least profoundly transformed, as these sectors require onerous labours to satisfy secondary needs. Products or "services" like the telephone, and the electricity that is currently being used for the most part by businesses, will be largely redirected to individual consumption. Buildings and machines can be put to different uses. Numerous needs will be satisfied with a minimum expenditure of social labour.

Transportation, for example, will be based upon a more rational use of individual or collective vehicles. The "demand" for punctuality will be greatly relaxed. The need to travel will arise much less frequently.

Many activities will not simply be completely abandoned but will instead be profoundly transformed. Education will escape to the greatest degree possible all capitalist influence. The press will cease to be the tool of the big newspapers in order to be made available to a multitude of publishers of small newsletters.

The essence of the new society will no longer consist in producing and competing in order to preserve market share, but in reducing arduous and boring industrial labour as much as possible.

The closure of useless sectors will allow for the variation and amelioration of those productive tasks that will still be necessary. The social forces thus liberated will be able to engage in new activities.

Children, students, the elderly and housewives will be able to participate according to their abilities in social activities; this participation will no longer take the form of competition on the "labour market".

These transformations are not luxurious baits the revolution will use to attract doubters. They are immediately necessary for combat and to concentrate forces against that portion of capital that poses the threat of temporary resurgence.

Science and Automation

All of these measures only give us a vague idea of what is to come. Communism will use the material basis bequeathed from the old world. It will above all develop the technological and scientific achievements of the latter. And it will do so more rapidly and better.

It is fashionable to express surprise at the technological progress achieved after the last world war. In fact, one would be more justified to express surprise at the slowness with which scientific discoveries have penetrated industry. The latter is characterized, in principle, by its inertia. It advances when historical "accidents" force it to change its suppliers and markets, and when it modifies its technical basis when interest rates fall, in order to try to escape from economic stagnation.

Contemporary industry functions by finding new uses for inventions and discoveries made decades ago. For example, vehicles based on the combustion engine and petroleum-based fuels, such as our state of the art automobiles, are veritable fossils compared with the scientific possibilities.

Industry has not really been able to make much progress with regard to either the automobile or new sources of energy. Nor can it do so unless such an effort is profitable from its narrow point of view.

Communism will allow for the construction of machines or industrial facilities that would be unprofitable from the point of view of the single enterprise or even of a capitalist state. Communism will judge that the achievement of progress is worth the effort even if it does not confer any immediate advantages. It will often perceive such advantages where capitalism was blind to them: increasing the quality of products, spurring interest in research, and improving working conditions, for instance.

From the capitalist point of view it would not be profitable to manufacture a silent jackhammer since the price of such an invention would not be less than or equal to that of a noisy jackhammer. It is of little importance to the capitalist that an economy of this kind has to be paid for with such obvious inconveniences. The fact that some day the production of a silent jackhammer could be perfected in such a manner as to become less expensive than the noisy jackhammer. This does not enter into the projections made when the product is offered for sale. Why should a business risk bankruptcy or any kind of sacrifice in the name of technical progress or the betterment of humanity? Communism will not be content to just take over from capitalism and carry on with business as usual. It will transform science and technology. From conscious or unconscious servants of the industrial hell, it will transform them (science and technology) into instruments of human liberation.

Science will never again be a sector separate from production.

Capital has a vital need for innovation. It cannot cause it to arise directly from the productive sector. The latter must proceed smoothly and the imagination must by no means be given free reign. Science is carried on elsewhere.

For many years science was marginal; it was the work of dedicated amateurs. Capital had a great need for their services and took them under its wing. Under the tutelage of the State and industry, science became an investment. It became bureaucratized, and came under the control of mandarins and managers. The freedom of creation was corralled.

In the eyes of scientific opinion, this can be good or bad. The man of knowledge is the sorcerer transformed into a wage worker. What is actually the result of the spirit of critical inquiry appears to popular opinion as magic.

The ideology of production recuperates what it had to concede to the experimental impulse. Science appears as the sector where a special commodity is produced: Knowledge. Knowledge ceases to be the delicate result of specialized research in order to be transformed into a sacralised product offered up for the contemplation of a mass of mental defectives.

For us it is a question of liberating the impulse of initiative and experimentation so that these qualities will come within the reach of all. Science will no longer be the exclusive possession of a caste of specialists and will instead once again be the taste for risk and play, the pleasure of discovery.

The "conquest" of space has illustrated the possibilities of automation and electronics. All that is necessary is to apply all this technology to everyday life, to the transformation of our daily life. Automation will allow humans to be disencumbered of boring jobs, which will be mechanized.

The first steps of automated systems—systems that, once set in motion, can function and operate without human intervention—were taken during the times of the Pharaohs. They were used to regulate the floodwaters of the Nile. With the passage of time such systems began to flourish. The first automated "factories" appeared. There was, for example, the mill invented and displayed near Philadelphia which in 1784 received wheat and turned it into flour without human intervention. Along with automated machines for production, calculating machines were also developed. In 1881 the telephone was invented.

Automation in this sense has existed for a long time. It is nothing but an extreme form of machine production. Electronics will allow such automation to become more widespread and even an ordinary form of machine production.

The electronics associated with the control of important sources of energy will allow action to be conducted at a distance and the centralization of a great number of operations.

Automation not only represents the promise of transferring painful or distasteful tasks to machines. It also, and perhaps most importantly, represents the possibility of doing things that would have otherwise remained impossible. It makes possible operations that require very fast reactions and very complicated calculations that surpass human abilities. Machines can operate in conditions that are hostile to life. Without automation the development of nuclear energy or space travel would have been impossible.

Those who want revolution but reject the

accursed science and technology are in a dead-
end. The massive destruction of our natural
environment is certainly not unconnected with
technological possibilities but one cannot blame
them for it either.

Nuclear energy or computer science can
present very dangerous characteristics. This is the
reflection of their power. But these aspects are
prejudicial to society only insofar as they are used
carelessly or are employed for the purpose of
reinforcing social control.

Up until now capitalism has only applied
automation to this or that detail of the system. This
does not imply that it can stop here. Its logic, the
need to bolster or to find an appropriate rate of
profit, commits it to continual advance. By this we
do not mean to suggest that the generalization of
automation is compatible with the preservation of
the current system. Automation's very principles are
contrary to the survival of class society: it renders
the proletariat useless.

"Automated machinery ... represents the exact
economic equivalent of slave labour" (Norbert
Wiener). The logical result of the development of
automated production would make the human
machines superfluous.

The solution is therefore either the communist

revolution or the annihilation of the proletariat, who would be reduced to a layer of refugees or else totally eliminated. The prophets of doom have predicted the latter outcome. Our optimism is not based on the humanity of our masters: history has shown us that those who carry out genocide have absolutely no hesitation to do so. We believe that they are simply incapable of exercising control over the situation and implementing a consistent policy. For good or for ill we are not governed by supermen but simply by veritable cretins, skilled at manipulation but incapable of viewing events from a historical perspective. They are themselves in part separated from the productive process. The really decisive point with regard to this question is that the proletariat must not prove to be too weak.

The proletarians dispose of an immense force. Their degree of consciousness of this force is extremely slight. The working class always possesses its force in the place it occupies in the productive apparatus. The first stirrings of automation have only strengthened this force. Small teams of workers and technicians hold enormous power in their hands. Economic upheavals can instil them with the inclination to use it.

The bourgeoisie and the bureaucracy cannot negate the proletariat without also negating themselves. They are chained to value, which is to say that they are chained to the human labour power that forms the basis of value. They do not seek progress for the sake of progress but only for the sake of money. If they develop machine production this is only because they want to free themselves of workers who are too unruly. The proletariat is not just a simple tool of the ruling class but also the latter's reason for existence. Capital (or labour) relegates man to the level of the machine but cannot cease to be a social relation between classes.

Class Society and Robotics

All class society tends to turn man into a robot, to reduce him to an object whose body and mind are used. When part of society does not work for itself but toils to feed another part of society, this implies that it must perform supplementary labour but also, and even more importantly, that the nature of its activity has changed. What is of interest to the master is not the pleasure or the pain, the happiness or the punishment of the slave, but his productive output. Class society is based on the human possibility of creating goods that can be separated from their producers in order to be used by others. The human being is no longer a human being but a tool. The innately human capacity to make tools and decide in advance what is to be produced is turned against man in order to transform him into a tool.

The exploiter can be kind or cruel to the exploited. The former does not have to be totally without any feelings. Rather, feelings are necessary to grease the wheels of the system. But they are limited and secondary products of the system. The exploiter can be "good" but he cannot cease to exploit. He can be a sadist but he cannot destroy his human material. Where capitalism does reach such a condition, however, it is under great economic pressure.

The ruling classes of the past preyed upon the agrarian communities. These communities were destroyed in order to bring a mutilated and atomized human material under their rule. One commodity among others, the proletariat came face to face in the market of "factors of production" with its mechanical competitors. In this war the machine won one battle after another and conquered space in the productive process from the proletariat.

Communism will transform the nature of this development. Man will not compete with the machine because he will no longer be a "factor of production".

The communist use of machine technology signifies the possibility of applying automation to a great number of activities. This is not to say that generalized automation will be the key to the "social question", however.

The abolition of wage labour does not mean the replacement of man by machine but the transformation of human activity in a human sense by means of machines. It is not merely a question of the gradual or sudden reduction of the working week from forty hours to zero. A world in which an entirely automated industry working on an inexhaustible raw material supplies him with everything desirable and imaginable would lead man to a vegetative condition. It would be a frozen world and without a sense of adventure since all that happens would be programmed in advance.

Regardless of the faith put in science, this myth is deeply capitalist. It considers as natural a complete separation between work time and leisure time. It wants to reserve the hell of production machinery and the paradise of consumption for humans. Depending on how strictly the limits to such a process were set, it would lead to either a permanent Club Med or the generalization of the condition of a foetus.

Communism is the end of the separation

between labour time and free time, between production and consumption, between life and experience.

Remuneration

The disappearance of the wages system is sufficient to shake the foundations of the old society. The compulsion to work in order to survive will disappear. Labour will no longer be a means of earning a livelihood. It will no longer be an intermediate term between man and his needs. It will be the direct satisfaction of a need. In this sense it will no longer be labour. What impels a person to action will cease to appear as a necessity that is external to the individual in order to become instead an internal necessity: the desire to do something, the will to be useful. This dissociation of activity and remuneration, if by remuneration one does not mean the pleasure that such activity can concretely provide, must proceed hand in hand with a profound transformation of man: it asks individuals to take responsibility for what they do, it requires that they develop intelligence and initiative and that egoism and mean-spiritedness should disappear.

It is customary to explain all the evils of humanity by the incorrigibility of human nature.

Everyone knows that man is a wolf to man. This explains nothing but demonstrates the kind of contempt that human beings have for themselves. It is the reflection of the fatalism that capitalism engenders by reducing the human being to the role of a spectator to his own development.

The idea that we should preserve some kind of remuneration for a transitional period, as Marx proposed, in the form of a distribution of coupons reflecting hours worked, is not desirable. If it is the development of the productive forces that makes the communist revolution possible, and today it certainly does, then the revolution cannot delay the full application of its principles. A system of coupons for remuneration and therefore to compel men to work would be a contradiction of the spontaneous revolt of the oppressed, of all those who participated in the insurrection without any expectation of power, or money, or compensation of any kind. A system of coupons would only have the sympathy of bureaucrats, leaders, and of all those who would like to exercise control and power over others. Such a system would only have the effect of dampening the ardour of the active elements and would not attract the opponents of action. If it becomes necessary in a particular case to make someone do something we would prefer the method of the kick in the ass. It is more straightforward and more effective.

We are not totally opposed in principle to the use of coupons. It would be absurd to allow diamonds to be subject to free distribution! In such cases the relevant authorized committees will allocate the coupons. When the goods in question are production goods, a factory council will allocate the coupons. When the coupons are for rare or dangerous medicines the hospitals or doctors will allocate them ... these coupons will not serve the purpose of remuneration. They will fulfil the role that is currently fulfilled by a medical prescription. More generally, the coupons' use will be determined by the nature or by the scarcity of the goods for which they will be "exchanged".

Most of the goods subject to distribution, especially food, must be distributed at no cost and with no restrictions under the auspices of the revolutionary committees and councils in the revolutionary zones or by means of expropriations in the non-liberated zones. This is the simplest, the least costly and the most pleasant method of distribution. It is the most suitable method for popularizing communism. It is advisable to apply this as a general rule, with the exception of rigorous action against abuses resulting from petty enforcement of complicated rules and from dissatisfaction with distribution norms.

Laziness

Won't such a program be an invitation to mass laziness? If it were possible to abolish the principle of remuneration for labour while simultaneously preserving the world as it is today, this would most assuredly be true. Communism, however, transforms the conditions of life and work in their entirety.

The revolutionary spirit is not a spirit of sacrifice: each individual forgetting himself in order to serve the collectivity. This is not communism—it is Maoism! Communism presupposes a certain degree of altruism but it also presupposes a certain degree of egoism. Above all, it does not oppose love for one's neighbour to love for one's self, asking each individual to serve his neighbour. We don't love either the priests or the scroungers. It is capitalism that causes the interest of the individual and that of the collectivity to be constantly opposed to each other: to give is to renounce.

Communist man will be neither the man of self-abnegation nor the man who submits to fate. The spiritual transformation that accompanies communism will not be a mere substitute for education. There will be no ideal image to which one must conform. There will be no separation between the transformation of social structures, on the one hand, and the transformation of individuals, on the other. It is capitalism that separates things like that. The proletariat will dis-alienate itself and can only do so by changing the world and its conditions of existence. A few weeks of revolution will shatter decades of conditioning. Cowardice, greed and weakness of character are the results of a certain kind of social condition. Deception, the truncheon, or education will only be capable of making people reject such base characteristics if the situation that engendered them and made them seem useful does not disappear. With communism these kinds of approaches will disappear because their corresponding objects have disappeared.

If there are egoists, incurable slackers and irremediable incompetents they will not necessarily pose a serious threat. The greatest enemy of such people is not repression but boredom. The least avid of them will surrender. Men are social animals. They lack the courage to be useless in a collectivity where they live. Even today the parasite and the egoist have to dissimulate. Once the system of wage labour is abolished it will be hard to nourish illusions about one's activity. Each person will be judged not by the time spent on some task but by what they really accomplish.

Communism does not exclude disagreements between individuals and groups. Slackers risk being asked to account for themselves. If they are supported and allowed to fatten themselves at the expense of the community that is because the community wants it that way.

Communists have nothing against a healthy laziness. The revolutionary society was not created so that we can work ourselves to the bone. We have no problem with the lazy person who does not demand from others what he rejects for himself. We don't mind if some high-spirited individuals play their practical jokes, as long as they don't try to impose their personal tastes on everybody!

By replacing compulsory labour with passionate activity the majority of the causes of systematic laziness will disappear. Gone too will be the irritation that the workaholic feels when he sees someone goofing off, which is often nothing but disguised envy.

Those who are lazy today are not necessarily those who will be lazy in the world of tomorrow. Among the latter will be those who now exert themselves to exhaustion in the pursuit of profits; they will need to be watched carefully.

In an established communist society, machinery will grant man great power. Each person will be able to choose his work rhythm. One person will devote great efforts to costly adventures and will spend more in terms of resources than he produces for society. Another will not do much and society will be in debt to him. Such debts shall not be subject to accounting.

Once the financial incentive has disappeared will the spirit of free inquiry and invention disappear as well? No one will be satisfied doing his job in a routine manner! It is a mistake to think that the desire for profit and the spirit of free inquiry go hand in hand. The merchant negotiates using the lie and illusion. The scientist must always reject both. Science makes its contribution and the invention makes money but there is often a discrepancy between those who discover and those who profit. Even in the capitalist world the motor of scientific passion is not money. Creativity and imagination are recuperated for the purpose of making money.

Allocation of Tasks

By allowing laziness doesn't our society run the risk of collapsing into chaos? Even if good will generally prevails, will it be enough to regulate the coordination of all necessary activities? Won't everybody rush to try to get an easy job and abandon the hard jobs before machinery is developed to perform the latter? In short, each person, by doing what he wants, will lead the whole world to catastrophe!

The view that modern society is very complicated and that this complexity is inevitable is very common. This is not just an illusion. The individual feels lost in the capitalist jungle. He does not identify with it, much less understand how it functions as a whole. It is a mistake, however, to think that this impression would apply to any modern society. This idea is not necessarily due to the multitude of operations and relations that constitute society as a whole. It originated in the separation of the function of decision and coordination, on the one hand, and execution, on the other.

This impression of complexity and permanent disorientation that capitalist society produces has influenced some depictions of the socialist world of the future. It is widely believed that the main problem that has to be solved in the society of the future is that of planning and coordination. A "Plan Factory" has been imagined, an enterprise that is responsible for evaluating the state of the economy and determining the technical coefficients that express the relative inputs of one product in the production of another product: the quantity of coal needed to produce one ton of steel, for example. This "Factory" will propose attainable goals and assume responsibility for the necessary revisions as the plan is implemented. The problems of the future society are thus understood primarily as problems of management. (Chaulieu (Castoriadis), *Socialisme ou Barbarie* No. 22)

The communist society will also have complex problems to solve. The resolution of these questions will not be the purview of any particular committee or group. There is nothing to be gained from an attempt to predict the forms that human activity will take, but only in the determination of its content. It will no longer be necessary to unite or to manage something that will no longer be separate and scattered. The free producer will address himself to both his own activity and his connections with the totality of general needs and possibilities.

In the revolutionary society relations between men will be clear and transparent. The fear of competition that renders the trade secret compulsory will disappear. What is essential is not that every person should attain competence in universal science and that every brain should be a "Plan Factory" in miniature. What good does it do me to know where the minerals came from that were used to manufacture my fork! What matters is that the necessary information should circulate freely and should be available.

In a fluid society where the spirit of individualism and enterprise patriotism will have disappeared, where each person will have many useful skills, individuals and groups will be oriented towards the fulfilment of the needs of society.

Social needs will not be imposed from the outside by means of a centralized office: whether a democratic assembly or a dictatorial committee. The individual or the group will no longer have to submit to their consciousness of the situation if we imagine this consciousness as a simple reflection of external imperatives. We shall act safely in recognition of our consciousness of social needs and possibilities but not independently of our own tastes and inclinations. Often, no compromises will be necessary. We shall perceive in social needs our own aspirations. We shall be more inclined to apply a remedy where we perceive a deficiency. If I lack wine it will not be necessary for me to acquire information regarding the details of production on a computer in order to deduce that perhaps the vines need to be tended!

The communist man of the future will not separate

the fulfilment of his tastes from its social impact. He will not throw himself into tasks that someone else has already attended to. In any event it would be stupid to think that the whole world should be standardized and that those who work the same jobs should follow the same fashion trends.

There will be a more acute awareness of what society needs than is now the case. The whole world will be able to be informed about and will be capable of understanding what works and what does not work, even if it does not have a direct effect on everybody. Computers will be essential tools for the circulation and interpretation of information.

Society's general organization has absolutely no need for either one or several central planning offices. Perhaps there will be certain individuals who will be responsible for gathering data, and drawing up projections for the future, but they will not have to elaborate a "plan" in the compulsory sense of the word. Such planning would amount to a desire to chain the future to the present!

Coordination will not be the permanent job of a particular caste. It will be carried out continuously at all levels of society. Because men will not be separated by a thousand barriers, they will spontaneously associate.

This is not to say that everything will go

smoothly. Conflicts will be inevitable. But the task of the revolution is not to liberate society from all kinds of conflict and thus to bring about a society where everything is harmonized "a priori". Certain kinds of conflicts will be utterly eliminated, those which sundered social classes and nationalities, for example.... In the world we want there is a place for both agreement and opposition. Harmony and equilibrium will be brought about by way of discussion and debate.

The basic difference with regard to the current situation is that in the future society each individual can only rely on his own personal forces in a conflict. There will be no appeal to abstract rights derived from the world of conflicts and concrete relations of force. The opportunity to resort to a specialized social force like the army or the police in order to impose the "recognition" of the truth of a cause will not be possible.

Communism will transform conflict into something normal and necessary, subject to the obvious condition that the possible gains from conflict outweigh the damage it incurs. Capitalism is profoundly conflict-ridden. It is based upon the opposition between classes, nations and individuals. It is a battle of all against all. Love and "fraternity" were preached in order to exorcise this reality. Aggression rules all, but the image of "peace" must reign. If someone must be killed it is not done in the name particular interests but for the advancement of civilization, for universal values, etc....

Doesn't a communist society run the risk of wasting a great deal of time in talk and debate? This is a risk we can take, considering the scale of the problems of coordination and adjustment. The idea that time is something that can be lost or gained is itself somewhat odd. From the communist point of view the problem cannot be narrowly focused on discovering which method achieves the best economy of time. What matters is the way this time is used.

Will people get pleasure and become interested in debates and attempts to bring about harmony, or would they prefer to be satisfied with implementing without debate the decisions of an executive committee that will have arranged that there will be no opposition? Men will learn how to debate and polemicize in a way they find pleasant. The more tedious debates will be limited by the boredom of the participants but also by the simple fact that many things do not have to be debated, for we can rely on past experience.

Undesirable Jobs

There are some jobs that are frankly nasty and unpleasant. We hope to reduce their number with the use of machinery, but until then they will still have to be done; nor can we eliminate all of them.

It would be unacceptable, and would not in any case be accepted by those involved, for these bad jobs to always be done by the same persons. It will be necessary to allocate them among the greatest number of persons who will take turns doing them. The resulting loss of efficiency will be a matter of secondary importance.

In the factories and other productive facilities we will be able to peacefully divest ourselves of unpleasant jobs.

At the level of society as a whole these bad jobs will also be subject to the principle of rotation of personnel. Everyone will have at least one assignment each year as a garbage collector.

The impact of the bad jobs will seem much less when compared to the time spent on pleasant activities. Today jobs are extremely specialized, as the requirements of the "rational" use of labour power demand that each worker should do one particular routine and leave the rest for other workers. In communist society the researcher will be able to participate in cleaning the lab he uses, the driver will be able to help pave the roads, and who is better-placed than the dead man to dig his own grave?

Disagreeable activities will be much less disagreeable if those who do them only devote a small part of their time to them, and do not labour under the impression—as is now the case—that they will be chained to them their whole life. Above all, such activities can be carried out in an environment quite different from the one they take place in today: without harassing foremen, without the obsession for profit. Garbage collection could, for example, take on a carnival-like aspect.

Many undesirable jobs are considered as such not so much by virtue of their actual nature as due to the fact that, in the name of the rationalization of labour, they are executed in mass production and always by the same persons.

These transformations in the rhythm, the distribution and the very nature of jobs will not be programmed in advance and planned from "above". They will be carried out in the workplace in the context of the desires of the people involved. If someone involved in a particular productive process is passionately attached to driving a forklift or some other task that is not generally held in high esteem, it would obviously be absurd to deprive him of his pleasure.

We are not fanatics of equality. It would be stupid if, with surgeons in short supply, we forced them to work as nurses. Such inequalities cannot be attenuated except by means of the retraining and transfer of people to truly useful sectors.

The End of Separations

Communism means the end of the separations that compartmentalize our lives.

Work life and emotional life will no longer be opposed. There will no longer be separate times for production and for consumption. Schools, production facilities, sites for entertainment ... will no longer be distinct and separate universes with nothing in common. They will gradually disappear with the disappearance of their specialized functions. Within the productive process, hierarchical divisions and the fragmentation of human activities will be confronted. This will mark the end of the situation where the worker is the executor of the designer, the designer the executor of the engineer, the engineer the executor of the financial department or management.

Bringing these changes to fruition will take some

time. We cannot immediately erase our current way of life, or our type of technological development, or certain human customs and defects. We shall nonetheless immediately implement measures to initiate this process and to make its effects felt by abolishing commodity production and the wages system.

The separation of one's work life on the one side and one's emotional and family life on the other is linked to the development of wage labour. The peasant was uprooted from his land and his family to be integrated into the industrial universe. Previously, the family constituted the unity of life and of production. The man and his wife, but also the children and the elderly, participated in farm labour and gathered wood. Each person found something useful to do that was within his capacities.

Reactionaries like to defend the endangered "family". These cretins just cannot understand that it is precisely the order they defend that transformed the family into what it is today. Kinship ties were elements of mutual aid in the agricultural world. They extended beyond the immediate family and its direct descendants. Today the family is only the place where babies are produced—and sometimes not even babies: its economic role is that of a unit of consumption! The basic institution, the elemental cell of highly developed capitalist society, is not the family, but the business enterprise.

It is not our intention to restore the old patriarchal family so it can take over production from the capitalist enterprise. Blood ties were capable of playing a great role in the past. They no longer play such a role in the modern world.

In communist society, in order to carry out productive or non-productive activity, people will not be brought together by the power of capital. We shall associate freely in accordance with our shared tastes and affinities. Relations between persons will be as important or even more important than production itself.

We are not claiming that occupational and amorous connections will exactly coincide. This will be a matter of choice and of chance. It will be much more likely than it is now.

Some people wish to depict communism as a system that makes women and children common property. This is stupidity.

Amorous relations have no other guarantee than love. Children will not be tied to their parents by the need to eat. The feeling of ownership over persons will disappear along with the feeling of ownership over things. This is very disturbing to those who need the guarantee of the priest or the judge. Marriage will disappear as a state-sanctioned sacrament. The question of whether two or three... or ten people want to live together or even enter into an agreement to do so is nobody's business but their own. We shall not determine or limit in advance the forms of sexual relations that are possible, healthy or desirable. Even chastity will not be totally rejected. It is a perversion that is just as worthy as any other! What is important, besides the pleasure and the satisfaction of the couple, is that the children live in an environment that responds to their need for material security and affection. This is not something that can be left to morality.

Hypocrisy rules over the remains of the family putrefied by the commodity. Love is said to exist where there is actually nothing but economic or emotional security or sexual gratification. Relations between parents and children have reached the pit of degradation. Under the veil of affection the will to exploit answers the desire for possession. The birth of a child burdens the parents with worries about the child's future. The child must play with his toys, get good grades in school, and show that he is intelligent and well behaved, alert and full of initiative. In exchange he receives a little affection or pocket money.

The family, in need of security and love

in a cold, hard world, is not immune to the commercialized reality in the workplace, where the expenditure of too much emotion is avoided. The superficial amiability and constant handshaking conceal contempt, rivalry and exploitation. Everyone is good, everyone is friendly, everyone communicates, but above all everyone is terribly annoyed by each other's presence.

Production and Consumption

The separation of production from consumption appears to be a natural division between two very distinct spheres of social life. Nothing could be more false. This can be viewed from two angles.

First, the frontier between what is called production time and consumption time is quite mobile when considered historically, and quite confused when considered in its ideological dimension. In which category should we put cooking, or sports? It depends on whether those involved are professionals or amateurs. The cardinal point is not the nature itself of the activity: cooking is more productive than the postal service in the sense that it presupposes a material transformation, whether or not those engaged in it are paid wages.

Many activities that pertain to consumption

have fallen under the sign of production. The astronaut or the invalid who breathes from an oxygen tank and the housewife, who buys ground coffee or jars of jam, participate in the shifting of the frontiers between these two spheres.

The split between production and consumption conceals the continuing importance of unpaid housework in the modern world. It confers a fixed and natural appearance on a separation that is actually flexible and socially determined.

Secondly, all productive activity is also necessarily consumption. It does nothing but transform matter in a certain way and in a certain sense. At the same time that it destroys, or, if you prefer, consumes certain things, we obtain, or, if you prefer, we produce others. Consumption is productive; production is also consumption. Production and consumption are the two inseparable sides of the same coin.

The concepts of production and consumption are not neutral. It cannot be said that they are bourgeois. But bourgeois society uses them. A fruit tree is not bourgeois because it produces fruit. The notion of production assumes an ideological character because behind the idea of creation and growth lies the idea of consciousness and planning. The confusion of the two concepts is preserved.

Everything ends up being interpreted in the terms of production. A chicken becomes a factory to manufacture eggs.

The continuity of the cycle through which primitive or civilized, capitalist or communist man modifies the world in which he lives in a simple or an intelligent way, individually or collectively, irreversibly or temporarily, on a large scale or in minor details, and transforms himself as well, is thus disguised. The totalitarian use of the idea of production conceals the radical insertion in and dependence of the human being on his environment and natural laws. Everything is interpreted in terms of domination and instrumentality. Man the producer, self-conscious and self-controlled, starts with the conquest of nature. The vast power that humanity conferred upon the image of divinity can be directly attributed to humanity's own self-image. Communism is not the victory of consciousness over unconsciousness. It is not the stage in which, after having been devoted to the production of things, man will at last be able to produce himself, and take over in a way from the divine creator. To say that man will be his own master just as he is the master of the object that he produces is to seek to reunite what has been separated and thus separation itself under the sign of production. The producer will thus not cease to be an object; he will simply be his own object.

The split between production and consumption is confronted in order to abolish the separation—a separation that is concrete enough but arbitrary from the point of view of nature and psychology—between the time employed on making money and the time employed on spending it.

For the communist man consumption will not be opposed to production since there will no longer be a conflict between acting for oneself and acting for others. This is because by producing for others, he creates use values that can serve him as well. He will not produce shoes in order to later be obliged to buy them on the market. Above all, production will be transformed and it will become creation, poetry and potlatch. Groups or individuals will express themselves through their activity. In this respect the revolution is the generalization of art and its supersession as a separate commercial sector.

Extending our reflections within the context of the opposition between consumption and production, it can be said that by having found satisfaction and pleasure (or the opposites, dissatisfaction and displeasure) through his productive activity, man will be a consumer. The computer or the shovel he will use will not have a fundamentally different value from the automobile or the food that he will use at another time.

Communism is by no means production finally put at the service of the consumer, nor can it be, as is the case with capitalism, the dictatorship of production. By engaging in an activity, one will acquire a certain power. Up to a point one will be able to do what one wants with the fruit of one's labours, and give up or keep what one has produced. Above all, by providing this or that good or service and giving it a particular form, one will have an impact on the possibilities of society. The activity of the end-users will be determined by that of the producers. There is no incentive for the latter to abuse a power that by no means can assume the form of political or separate power but is the simple expression of the usefulness of their jobs.

The "consumer" will not be able to reproach the producer for the imperfection of what he does in the name of the money that he did not give in exchange, but will be able to simply criticize him not from the outside but from the inside. The object of his criticism will be their common labour if he participates in the same production process. If an individual is not satisfied with what the producer is doing or not doing he will not be able to appeal to his abstract rights as a consumer. He will have no other recourse than to oppose his own ability to do it better or at least to attempt to make his own suggestions or contributions prevail. Criticism will be impassioned and positive. It will not take the form of complaining and then not doing anything about it.

Production and Education

The separation between productive life and education is not the fruit of necessity. It cannot be explained by the increasing importance of knowledge and training. Instead we must understand why it is necessary for knowledge to no longer be the direct fruit of experience.

The basis of this split lies in the fact that the proletariat must not be able to attend to his own self-improvement, his pleasure or his education, when he is engaged in production. This separation that is so essential for the survival of the world of the economy comes at a very high price. It implies the immobilization of a major part of the population in schools, vocational training centres and universities who could be much more useful and have much more fun outside these institutions. This does not allow for the effective adaptation of human abilities to the requirements of the activities they must later undertake. This kind of *in vitro* training is complemented by an apprenticeship in the workplace that is often carried out secretly.

The education system is presented as a "public service" that is above the distinctions of social classes. We are supposed to take its usefulness for granted. Who would dare to be an apostle of ignorance? Enlightened minds attack the curriculum. They accuse it of being archaic, of being separated from real life, that it is contributing to subversion. According to their recommendations students should be taught to read the *Bible*, *The Communist Manifesto* or the *Kamasutra*!

The most extreme critics put the blame on the education system itself. They do not do so in the name of combating its deadly "efficiency", but rather its inefficiency! They take on the school in order to thereby defend pedagogy all the more effectively.

It is necessary to learn and to learn forever. To swallow this insipid paste called culture. The world is so complicated! You do not understand it? Then you need a "refresher course".

People have never before learned so much and never have they been so ignorant with respect to what concerns their own lives. They have been crushed, beaten to a pulp by the mass of information that oozes from the university, the newspapers, and the television. The truth will never come from the accumulation of commodity-knowledge. It is a dead knowledge that is incapable of understanding life because its nature is precisely to be separated from experience and real life.

The school is where one learns to read, to write and to add and subtract. But the school is above all else an apprenticeship in renunciation. That is where we learn to do what we do not want to do, to respect authority, to compete with our friends, to dissimulate, and to lie. That is where the present is sacrificed for the sake of the future.

Communism is the decolonization of childhood. There will never again be the need for a particular institution for education. Are you worried about how children will learn how to read? You should be more concerned about how they will learn how to speak.

The school dissociates and inculcates the dissociation of the effort or process of learning and its necessity. What matters is that the child learns to read because it is necessary to learn to read rather than to satisfy his curiosity or his love for books. The paradoxical result is that literacy is on the decline at the same time that the taste for reading and the real ability to read has been eliminated in most people.

In communist society the child will learn to read and write because he will feel the need to learn and to express himself. The world of childhood, because it will not be separated from the rest of the world and from social life in general, will engender in the child an imperative need to learn. He will learn to read and to write as naturally as he will learn to walk and talk. He will not do this entirely on his own. He will find that his older friends or his parents will help him. The difficulties he encounters will prove useful. By overcoming them he will learn how to learn. By not receiving knowledge in the form of a pre-digested baby food from the hands of a teacher, he will become accustomed to observing and listening, he will be capable of elaborating his understanding and making deductions on the basis of his experience. This will be the reward of real life as opposed to the educational or vocational programming of human beings.

Men will share their experience and will communicate their discoveries. The times and places for this sharing and communication will be chosen on the basis of their convenience. The form this relation will assume will not be determined in advance. It will depend on the content of the knowledge mutually exchanged by those interested in the topic. At the risk of displeasing the fanatics of intensive pedagogy, if 10 or 10,000 people want to know what one individual knows, the simplest solution would be to reinvent the lecture hall.

The modern interest in pedagogy reflects the fact that teaching methods are not imposed on the basis of a particular content. When there is no longer anything to say, the content of the lesson becomes interchangeable, and then the form of the lesson is debated. It is when the soup is bad that one becomes interested in how clean the bowl is.

What will happen in the world of capitalist production if the workers were to frequently really avail themselves of the right to experiment and were not judged by their immediate profitability? They would quickly forget why they were hired. They would get experience from their experiments, and their experiments would lead to further experience. By not producing they will quickly abandon efficiency in favour of pleasurable research, since no one is interested in what is being produced. The joy of discovery and the elation of freedom, total chaos and a festive atmosphere, will replace the repetitive routine. The contacts that will be developed among the workers under the pretext of improving production by means of the exchange of experience will be able to take new forms. Why not surrender to the intoxicating happiness of collective sabotage, why not organize games, why not reorganize and transform production in a way that would make it directly useful to the workers?

The principle of the system of wage labour militates against the possibility of trusting the workers, and instead subjects them to the requirements of a system of production that does not interest them. The most alienated, the most beaten down, and the most menial wage workers will not be retained by this slippery system. One cannot leave a worker to his own devices during the production process. If he is left on his own he will amuse himself by taking action against the capital that denies his humanity. He must be treated like a tool.

The capitalist division between production and training has its limits.

It is impossible to completely dissociate production, education and research. In production, even the least difficult job demands a certain degree of adaptability in the worker and the ability to deal with unforeseen circumstances. Similarly, the most abstract learning must find practical realization in some "product", even if it is a "crib" used to pass an examination. The necessity of external control has an impact on production.

The student is not a sheet of paper on which knowledge is inscribed. He will not be able to learn anything as long as he is completely passive. The period of apprenticeship cannot be totally separated from experience and the production process, even if it is separated from the strictly economic sphere. The school serves to provide a boundary and content to this limited activity and to disconnect it completely from real life. Teaching functions and continues to exist thanks to the principles it rejects. This is just as true of reading as it is of writing. Thus, the latter is the negation of all communication. The student must learn to express himself in writing, regardless of what he has to say and regardless as well of whom he is addressing(!).... It is a completely vacuous exercise. If the student writes, because he is forced to write, he will not be able to do so except by engaging in some type of communication. In this respect the student is like the worker who, compelled to work, can only carry out his assigned labour in collaboration up to a certain point. He cannot be a simple executor or machine.

The production system would collapse if the workers did not engage in experiments, if they did not assist one another, if they did not carry on discussions among themselves. The hierarchical organization of labour can only survive if its rules are constantly ignored. The hierarchical organization of labour imposes certain limits on these illicit and disrespectful activities as well as on the spontaneous activity of the workers in order to prevent them from spreading and becoming really subversive and a threat to the system.

5. Money and the Estimation of Costs

Communism is a world without money. But the disappearance of money does not signify the end of all evaluation of costs. The societies and human activities of the past, present and future are necessarily faced with this problem whether or not they use monetary symbols. The criteria selected for these evaluations obviously vary according to the essential nature of the society in question.

Money

In a highly developed capitalist society, where money has become the general equivalent for products, money appears in the eyes of all as a necessity even if everyone does not have the same amount and does not use it in the same way. It is a good that is almost as necessary for human life and almost as natural as oxygen. Can one survive without money? Both the rich and the poor have to reach for their wallets to cover their most essential needs or their most frivolous whims.

Corresponding to the objective, although limited, place occupied by money, there is the subjective and imaginary place occupied by money in the social consciousness. All wealth is eventually assimilated by monetary wealth by the servants of the economy. Things that have no price seem to lose all value even if they are the most indispensable goods required for life: air, water, sunlight, sperm and soap bubbles. Paradoxically, our era has finally, although in the sense that the triumphant commodity assumes responsibility for turning everything into a commodity value, bottled water and deposited sperm in a bank.

Where the vulgar are content with noting the ubiquity and the omnipotence of money and attempt to avail themselves of the favours of this capricious divinity, the learned economists assume responsibility for apologetics in its favour. Not only is money indispensable in today's society, and indeed is based upon an unfortunately undisputed everyday experience, but it is indispensable for all social existence that is even minimally civilized. Monetary circulation is to the social body what the circulation of the blood is to the human body. The history of progress is the history of the progress of money, from the primitive forms of money to today's letter of credit. Do you want to liberate society from money? You must be mentally retarded, an advocate of a return to barter. We may mention in passing that not only has capitalism not eliminated this much-discredited barter but has constantly reinvented it, notably at the level of international exchange.

Money has become a veil that has dissimulated economic reality. Gone are the milling machines, the engineers, spaghetti ... only dollars or roubles appear. It is always necessary for the control over money, its creation, its circulation and its distribution to correspond to an in-depth control of the entirety of use values into which the economy is converted. Hence the deception.

Money is often the focus of dissatisfaction but it is not the existence of money itself that arouses discontent but the parsimonious way it finds its way into our wallets. The more it is criticized, the more of it is demanded. Everyone wants to destroy the golden calf and abolish idolatry, but only in order to more effectively fill their own pockets. You have the choice between the brutalization of labour, the risk of getting mugged, and the randomness of the lottery....

Although the economists will object, we have to

say that money is a very strange thing. This becomes clear the moment that one ceases to think about it and its undeniable economic utility in order to focus instead on its usefulness for humanity.

Let us try to be naïve for a moment.

How is it possible, by what kind of infernal magic, that wealth, which makes possible the satisfaction of needs, has come to be interred in money? It was free to take any particular form to become visible, it could have appealed to our memories of the good times and to the example of Our Lord Jesus Christ, by choosing bread and wine which are things that are useful and agreeable. But, no! It preferred to embody itself in the form of gold and silver, which are among the most rare and least useful metals. Even worse, today it only shows itself to the common run of mortals in the form of paper.

The only need that money responds to is the need to exchange, and it will disappear with the disappearance of exchange.

It is monstrous to want to abolish money while preserving exchange or wanting to equalize exchange in all of its applications. During the early 19th century some "Ricardian Socialists" proposed that commodities should be exchanged directly with respect to the quantity of labour required for their production. The Bolsheviks Bukharin and

Preobrazhensky advocated the same illusion in 1919:

"Thus, from the very outset of the socialist revolution, money begins to lose its significance. All the nationalised undertakings, just like the single enterprise of a wealthy owner ... will have a common counting-house, and will have no need of money for reciprocal purchases and sales. By degrees a moneyless system of account-keeping will come to prevail. Thanks to this, money will no longer have anything to do with one great sphere of the national economy. As far as the peasants are concerned, in their case likewise money will cease by degrees to have any importance, and the direct exchange of commodities will come to the front once more.... The gradual disappearance of money will likewise be promoted by the extensive issue of paper money by the State.... But the most forcible blow to the monetary system will be delivered by the introduction of budget-books and by the payment of the workers in kind...."

– Nikolai Bukharin and Evgeny Preobrazhensky, 'The ABC of Communism', The University of Michigan Press, Ann Arbor, 1966, pp. 334-335

Attempts were made to at least partially de-monetize the economy by expressing transactions between enterprises only by means of quantifiable operations. Nothing very notable or very communist was thereby achieved.

Congratulations

In the communist world products will circulate without money having to circulate in the opposite direction. A balance will not be established at either the household or the enterprise level: all output of commodities will not correspond to an entry of money and vice-versa. It will be established directly in a comprehensive way and will be measured directly for the satisfaction of needs.

By the end of exchange we obviously do not mean that children will no longer be able to trade marbles or baseball cards or affectionate caresses. A limited degree of barter will subsist on a small scale. Above all at the beginning it will fill gaps in the general network of production and remedy any of its rigidities.

The best proof that the secret of money does not lie in its material nature is that monetary standards have changed according to time and place. Salt and cattle were once able to play this role. The precious metals, notably gold, were finally selected only due to their uselessness. In a time of scarcity gold cannot be withdrawn from circulation and consumed. When gold is withdrawn from circulation in order to be hoarded or to be used in ornamentation this is a result of its economic value. Its qualities and above all its rarity have given it priority at a certain level of economic development. In the first stage of the commodity system salt could be used as money due to its usefulness and due to the fact that its sources were concentrated in certain locations. It was the perfect object of circulation.

Today money demonstrates a tendency towards dematerialization. Its value is no longer backed by any other particular commodity but by the banking and financial system that control and manipulate it. It is still a means of exchange but has become above all an instrument at the service of capital. This allows it to be managed and utilized adequately to finance investments, and to provide credit to capital.

The destruction of money does not mean burning banknotes and confiscating or melting down gold coins. Such measures may be necessary for symbolic or psychological reasons, in order to disorganize the system. But they are not enough. Money would reappear under other forms if the need for and the possibility of money were to persist. Wheat, canned sardines, sugar ... could be means of exchange and payment for labour. "You do this work, I will give you ten kilos of sugar with which you can obtain meat, alcohol or a straw hat."

The problem is, first of all, that of the struggle for production, for organization, against scarcity. Next comes the enactment of repressive and dissuasive measures with respect to those who would seek to use the period of reconversion to operate on the black market. Gold and other precious materials will be requisitioned by the revolutionary authorities so as to eventually be ... exchanged with those sectors not yet under revolutionary control, for arms and for subsistence goods.

Money is the expression of wealth, but of commodity wealth. It is not itself the direct satisfaction of needs, but the means to satisfy them. It is therefore also the wall that separates the individual from his own needs.

The aspirations of men are the reflection of the things, the commodities that confront them. To have needs and to satisfy them is to be capable of buying and consuming. In this game one can only be swindled. Wealth, real happiness, cannot be acquired and must be publicly displayed as an unattainable dream.

The Law of Value

Money is used for exchange. But money also signifies measurement. What money measures in exchange, the price of the commodity, has its origin outside the sphere of exchange.

How is an equilibrium established, within the capitalist system, between what is produced and what is consumed? Between the effort expended and the benefit obtained? How is one choice determined to be more rational than another?

The problem applies to each particular commodity, which is a use value and an exchange value at the same time. The use value is the benefit that the commodity can supply. The consumer is thought to be able to directly assess this use value. Exchange value, expressed in the price, corresponds to the expense for which this good is purchased. It takes the form of monetary expenditure for the buyer but is above all and in principle an expenditure of labour.

The price of a good is determined by the forces that are exercised at the level of the market, by supply and demand. Beyond this aspect, however, price refers to the cost of production that is expended in labour directly utilized and in the labour contained in the materials used for production.

Each commodity therefore expresses the need for an equilibrium between the social expenditure and the social profit, which is reflected in the need for a financial equilibrium between business enterprises and households. The need for an equilibrium, but not of exactly that equilibrium! A good's price only corresponds in a very distorted way to the quantity of real labour effectively expended in its production and likewise to the socially necessary quantity of labour needed for its production. Equilibrium is not established at the level of the individual commodity but at the level of the system as a whole. And here this equilibrium is rather a kind of disequilibrium.

So, is the price of a commodity determined by the quantity of labour that it contains? Yes and no. Yes, because price has a tendency to vary in proportion to the increase of productivity, because a product that requires twice the time to produce than another runs the risk of costing twice as much, because the total mass of labour determines the total value of commodities. No, because one cannot establish a necessary and direct link between each commodity and the labour it contains. And this is true because if the price of a commodity were actually to be determined by the concrete labour crystallized in it, then the lower the productivity, the lazier the workers and the more expensive the commodity! In reality, those that have high cost prices are not at all favoured on the market. Those that win the market competition are those that economize on the costs of production and labour. And this is so because the formation of prices is affected by the tendency towards the establishment of an average rate of profit.

What then remains of the law of labour-value inherited from the classical economists that says that the value of things is determined by the labour contained in them? This law is a general law that, by means of the formation of prices, determines the general developmental trends of the system. Capital expands and is distributed as a result of the economies of labour time that it can realize. Like a river, even if its path is not the shortest route, even if it meanders in oxbows, even if it has many bends, finally it blindly follows its natural slope by destroying everything that stands in its way. The unnoticed profit that capitalism generates in order to invest here or there, to choose this or that technology or machinery, far from contradicting this tendency is nothing but the tortuous path by which it is imposed.

Finally, the law of value does not refer so much to the connection between the commodity and its price on the one hand, and on the other between the creative labour and its dissociation. By converting labour into value, the particular task is separated from labour and from the worker in order to be situated as a satellite in economic space, in which it moves according to its own laws. When all the commodities become autonomous and compete with each other they end up by obtaining the value among themselves by way of exchange and by means of money. With communism, the law of value disappears, a law whose development was intimately bound with that of exchange and that of the latter's influence on human activity.

What about the global equilibrium between expenses and income within the system itself? This equilibrium is a disequilibrium. From the point of view of value society produces more than it spends. The surplus is accumulated. Without this capital would not be capital.

Marx has shown that there is a special commodity that has the property of producing more value than is required for its production. This explains why capital in motion grows, from transaction to transaction, instead of remaining the same. This commodity is labour power; its price, which is lower than the value it creates, is the wage. The difference is the surplus value.

The worker does not sell his labour on what

is falsely called "the labour market", but his capacity to work, a part of his time. Labour is not a commodity; it has no value. It is the basis of value. Labour, Engels said, has as much value as gravity has weight.

When capital emerges from the sphere of circulation in order to enter the den of realization, the expenditure of the unpaid labour of the workers is increased, without which the law of value would be a joke; if this were not so then profit would appear to arise from mere price gouging or else would have to break with the laws of exchange. Each commodity-capital can be broken down into constant capital, which corresponds to the amortization of the raw materials and machinery utilized, variable capital, which corresponds to the wages, and surplus value or added value, which corresponds to unpaid labour.

Money is the bearer of a profound mystification. It conceals the original nature of the expenditure that really created the product. Behind wealth, even mercantile wealth, are nature and human effort. Money seems to produce interest, it seems to breed. The only source of value, however much it appears to derive from commerce and all the more so the more it does derive from commerce, is labour.

It is true that the most servile economists assign

a small place to labour as a source of wealth alongside capital and land. This does not even partially abolish the mystification. It is not labour as such to which this favour is conceded, it is labour as a counterpart of labour as an accounting entry. It is not money that is reduced to labour but the contrary, it is labour that is reduced, by way of the wage, to money.

Free Distribution

One might be tempted to conclude that, with the disappearance of money, communist society will no longer have to regulate costs, and that it will not have to calculate the value of things. This is a fundamental error.

The fact that a good or service is distributed free of charge is one thing. The assertion that this costs nothing is something else entirely. This illusion is a direct legacy of the functioning of the commodity system. We are accustomed to identify cost with payment. We only see the payment, the monetary expenditure. We overlook the expenditure in effort and materials that gave rise to the product in the first place.

In capitalism as well as in communism free distribution is not equivalent to the absence of costs.

The difference between communist free distribution and capitalist free distribution is that the latter is merely a semblance of free distribution; in the capitalist version, payment has not been eliminated, but has simply been deferred or shifted to another party. The fact that education and advertising are free does not mean that they are external to the commodity system and that the consumer does not ultimately pay for them. The freely distributed commodity is a very perverse thing. It implies an imposed or semi-imposed consumption, and hinders our ability to make choices and to refuse what is "offered" to us.

In the new society the cost of things will have to be ascertained and if necessary calculated in advance. Not because of a Manichaeism of accounting procedures or to avoid fraud, which will no longer have any reason to exist. It will be done in order provide the framework for deciding whether the particular expense incurred was justifiable, and to reduce it if at all possible. There will have to be an effort to assess the positive and negative effects on the human and natural environment of the satisfaction of a need or the implementation of a new project.

A needle, or a car—are the time and the effort devoted to their production as well as all the concomitant social costs of their use justified? Is it better to build a production facility in this location or somewhere else? Is a certain production process justified in consideration of its utilization of finite mineral resources? One cannot leave such things to chance or intuition. It is easy to see that all of this implies evaluation, calculation and forecasting.

If we retain the notion of cost, which is so redolent of economism, this is because it is not simply a matter of choice and measurement, an intellectual process, but a physical expenditure. Regardless of the technical level there will be activities that are more costly and jobs that are more arduous than others. It would be especially sad and strange if everything were to become easy and a matter of indifference in a communist society, even more so than it would be if this were to happen to other kinds of societies.

The commodity presents a double face: use value and exchange value. They seem to depend on two irreducible orders.

Use value, or utility, depends on the qualitative. The user compares and evaluates the airplane and the orange, in order to decide which would suit him better. The choice cannot be made independently of his situation and his concrete needs.

Exchange value depends on the quantitative.

Goods are all evaluated and objectively arranged in the framework of a single standard, whether the goods in question are airplanes or oranges.

Communism is not so much a world that perpetuates the realm of use value, finally liberated from the exchange value that parasitized it, as a world where exchange value is repudiated and becomes use value. Advantage and disadvantage come from the same order of things and are no longer either united or separated back to back. Value ceases to be value in order to reappear as concrete and diversified expenditure. Labour ceases to be the basis and the guarantee of value. There is no longer a single standard that allows for quantitative comparisons between all things, but concrete expenditures and labours, of various degrees of burdensomeness which should also be taken into account. Having ceased to perform its role as the basis of value unified by the exchange process, labour ceases to be LABOUR.

"The bourgeois economy is a double economy.

The bourgeois individual is not a man, but a trading company. We want to destroy all trading companies. We want to abolish the double economy in order to found a new one that is one single unit, which history already knew during the times when the cave man went to collect as many coconuts as there were comrades in his cave, with his hands as his only tools."

– Amadeo Bordiga, 'Property and Capital', 1950

Everything will be free because the "gift" will replace the act of selling. Those who carry out one or another kind of labour with the object of satisfying their own desires or being useful to others, will be paid directly by their own efforts.

Is this something new? No, since even today it never occurs to anybody to charge anyone else for the price of the saliva they used up in the course of a debate. In a conversation one does not exchange a certain time for speaking or a certain decibel level, one attempts to say what one has to say, because one feels that it has to be said. The interlocutor or the auditor does not owe us anything in exchange for their attention. Awaiting a response, the risk of running into incomprehension, silence, or the lie, are all part of the game. They are neither the expectation of payment nor the risks of the market. In everyday life the word is not a commodity; speaking is not a job.

What is true today of the word, when it is not recorded and sold as a commodity, will be true tomorrow for all of production. The estimation of the cost of production will no longer be distinct from the effort dedicated to its fulfilment. The very first step in this calculation will be the impulse that will lead towards this or that kind of activity. A book or a pair of shoes will be "offered" in the same way that words can be offered today. The gift implies, up to a certain point, reciprocity, the word implies the response, but this is no longer the anonymous and antagonistic process of exchange.

Labour Time

Since the time of Ricardo, the official economist of the English bourgeoisie, who during the early 1800s maintained that the value of a product was based on the quantity of labour necessary for its production, there has been no lack of people who demanded that the worker should receive the whole value of his product. Profit was morally condemned as theft. The problem of socialism was thus the problem of remuneration, of a fair day's pay.

An American communist, F. Bray, went even further. He saw equal exchange as not the solution, but a means for preparing the solution which is the community of goods. He envisioned a transitional period when no one could get rich by receiving only the value of his labour. Each worker would receive from the public warehouses the equivalent of what he had produced in the form of various objects. Equilibrium would therefore be maintained between production and consumption.

In *The Poverty of Philosophy*, Marx rendered homage to Bray but also criticized him. Either equal exchange leads to capitalism:

"Mr. Bray does not see that this equalitarian relation, this corrective ideal that he would like to apply to the world, is itself nothing but the reflection of the actual world; and that therefore it is totally impossible to reconstitute society on the basis of what is merely an embellished shadow of it. In proportion as this shadow takes on substance, far from being the transfiguration dreamt of, is the actual body of existing society."[/i] Or else it leads to exchange: *"What is today the result of capital and the competition of workers among themselves will be tomorrow, if you sever the relation between labour and capital, an actual agreement based upon the relation between the sum of productive forces and the sum of existing needs. But such an agreement is a condemnation of individual exchange...."*

– Karl Marx, 'The Poverty of Philosophy', Foreign Languages Press, Peking, 1978, pp. 70-72

Not wanting to resort to exchange, certain revolutionaries, Marx and Engels in the forefront, understood the imperious need to regulate the problem of costs and their accounting in the future society. They looked for a standard of measurement to evaluate and to compare costs.

The standard proposed has commonly been that of the quantity of labour. This quantity has been measured by time, corrected at times by taking the intensity of the labour into account. All of society's investments can in this way be reduced to a certain expenditure of time. The orange and the airplane no longer correspond to a certain quantity of money but to a given number of hours of labour. Despite the differences in their nature they can be compared according to the same scale of measurement.

This procedure seems logical. What could different goods have in common besides the labour they contain? This was where Marx started in [i] Capital when he was describing labour as the source of value. What other standard could be found?

Marx and Engels adopted this idea without pausing to consider the practical details. Others have tried to elaborate it in more detail, basing it upon a precise accounting of hours of labour, that would allow for the evaluation of every good produced.

For our part, we have not evoked the call to go "beyond labour" only to immediately fall back miserably upon the measurement of labour time, at the very moment when the time comes to tackle the really hard practical problems.

The theory of the measurement of goods or of the forecasting of investments by means of the quantity of labour is false. It must be radically rejected. This is not a methodological dispute but a basic problem that affects the very nature of communism itself.

Measurement by means of labour is still economistic. It seeks to bring about the end of the law of value but it does not take into account everything this implies. Capitalist society has a tendency to perpetuate itself even while unburdening itself of the division into classes and of exchange value!

A solution was sought to a problem that has two aspects. The first is that of the workers' pay. The second, more general, aspect concerns the distribution of the productive forces at the level of society as a whole.

How to distribute consumption goods without money? How to justly recompense the worker in view of the efforts he has contributed to production?

With respect to these questions Marx fell back in *The Critique of the Gotha Program* on the point of view of Bray, while purging it of its most tedious aspects. In a transitional period where the principle "to each according to his needs" still cannot be applied, remuneration will be based on the labour provided by each worker. It will only be based upon but not equivalent to it, since one part of what this labour represents must go to a social fund devoted to the production of production goods, support for invalids and the elderly, etc.... The worker cannot receive the full product of his labour. On the other hand, because the coupons that testify to the labour contributed by the worker do not circulate, exchange is totally destroyed at its source.

This is Marx's purpose in demanding that society should have some kind of accounting unit:

" ... labour, in order to serve as a measure, must be defined by its duration or intensity; otherwise it would cease to be standard."

– Karl Marx, 'Critique of the Gotha Program', in Marx: Later Political Writings, Cambridge University

Press, New York, 1996, p. 214

For Marx, the problem of remuneration is of secondary importance and only applies to the lower stage of communism. The question of the distribution of the productive forces, on the other hand, is of fundamental and permanent importance.

"On the basis of socialized production the scale must be ascertained on which those operations—which withdraw labour-power and means of production for a long time without supplying any product as a useful effect in the interim—can be carried on without injuring branches of production which not only withdraw labour-power continually, or several times a year, but also supply means of subsistence and of production."

– Karl Marx, 'Capital: Volume II', International Publishers, New York, 1967, p. 362

The calculation of necessary labour does not however imply that the law of value is perpetuated while money-capital disappears. The quantity of labour is allocated with reference to needs. In *The Poverty of Philosophy*, Marx wrote:

"In a future society, in which class antagonism will have ceased, in which there will no longer be any classes, use will no longer be determined by the minimum time of production; but the time of production devoted to different articles will be determined by the degree of their social utility."

– Karl Marx, 'The Poverty of Philosophy', Foreign Languages Press, Peking, 1978, p. 58

The law of value is nothing but an expression peculiar to commodity society of a more general rule that applies to every society:

"In reality, no society can prevent production from being regulated, in one way or another, by the labour time available to society. But insofar as this positing of the duration of labour is not effected under the conscious control of society—which would only be possible under the regime of communal property—but by the movements of commodity prices, the theory set forth with such precision in the Franco-German Yearbooks is completely vindicated."

That is what Marx wrote to Engels on January 8, 1868. What did Engels have to say with regard to this issue?

"As long ago as 1844 I stated that this balancing of useful effects and expenditure of labour on making decisions concerning production was all that would be left of the politico-economic concept of value in a communist society. [Deutsch-Französische Jahrbücher, p. 95] The scientific justification for this statement, however, as can be seen, was made possible only by Marx's Capital."

– Frederick Engels, 'Anti-Dühring', Foreign Languages Press, Peking, 1976, p. 403)

What Marx and Engels are telling us about communist society—and we see that they did have something to say about it!—follows directly from their analysis of capitalist society. Their ideas about the communist society of the future partake of both the assets and the deficiencies of their analysis of capitalist society.

The assets consist in demonstrating that the problems of the allocation of consumption goods and the remuneration of labour are not fundamental ones. It is the mode of production that determines the mode of distribution. To claim, contrary to the view of the beautiful souls, that the worker cannot receive the whole product of his labour, proceeds directly from an analysis of capitalism which shows that the value of a commodity represents, besides the wage and the surplus value, the constant capital. Instruments of production must be produced. Unlike previous social forms, capitalism and communism are societies provided with an abundance of tools.

Capitalism and communism are also societies undergoing constant change. There is no such thing as an unchanging condition. In these societies, it is not the case that everything is regulated in advance by reference to its past use and then eventually corrected by common sense. The estimation of costs is not so much a problem of accounting as a problem of forecasting. With regard to this fundamental point, there was a significant regression in the communists who came after Marx. Certain councilists would reduce the question to that of an almost photographic copy of reality and economic trends.

The following passage shows that, for Marx, today's society and the society of the future have to resolve the SAME problem. The former, thanks to money-capital and credit, and the latter, by dispensing with both.

"... on the basis of capitalist production, more extensive operations of comparatively long duration necessitate large advances of money-capital for a rather long time. Production in such spheres depends therefore on the magnitude of the money-capital which the individual capitalist has at his disposal. This barrier is broken down by the credit system and the associations connected with it, e.g., the stock companies. Disturbances in the money-market therefore put such establishments out of business, while these same establishments, in their turn, produce disturbances in the money-market."

"On the basis of socialised production the scale must be ascertained on which those operations — which withdraw labour-power and means of production for a long time without supplying any product as a useful effect in the interim — can be carried on without injuring branches of production which not only withdraw labour-power and means of production continually, or several times a year, but also supply means of subsistence and of production. Under socialised as well as capitalist production, the labourers in branches of business with shorter working periods will as before withdraw products only for a short time without giving any products in return; while branches of business with long working periods continually withdraw products for a longer time before they return anything. This circumstance, then, arises from the material character of the particular labour-process, not from its social form."

– Karl Marx, 'Capital: Volume II', International Publishers, New York, pp. 361-362

Marx and Engels placed too much emphasis on the continuity of communism with capitalism. This is their deficiency.

They preserve the bourgeois separation between the sphere of production and the sphere of consumption. Already in *The Manifesto*, they distinguished the collective property in the means of production from the personal appropriation of consumption goods. They thus emphatically affirmed that they did not want to socialize anything but what was already common social property: the instruments of capitalist production. In *The Critique of the Gotha Program*, Marx still opposed individual and family consumption to the labour time contributed to productive and social consumption. But he does not say how the latter will be established.

There is some confusion between the mode of distribution of the products and their nature as "consumption goods" or instruments of production. On the one hand are the individuals and on the other is society conceived abstractly. There are isolated individuals, individuals in groups, and individuals in communities, who confront one another and organize.

In reality, however, when the State or the owner of an enterprise as the representative of the "general interest" disappears, Society as separate from the individual also disappears. There are then nothing but isolated men, men in groups, and men in communities, who organize in this or that way. An individual can lay claim to a power tool and a neighbourhood committee to several tons of potatoes.

The separation between, on the one hand, labour power composed of separate individuals, and social and collective capital, on the other, will disappear. One cannot invoke the necessity for remuneration in a transition period to preserve this separation. To the contrary, the advocacy of this necessity in Bray or in Marx is the reflection of the limitations of an era when communism was still immature.

Despite his critical and pertinent observations, Marx was still dominated by the fetishism of time. Whether considered as an instrument of economic measurement or as an instrument of extra-economic measurement:

"For real wealth is the developed productive power of all individuals. The measure of wealth is then not any longer, in any way, labour time, but rather disposable time."

– Karl Marx, 'Grundrisse', Penguin Books, Baltimore, 1973, p. 708

Labour time is the basis of free time. The realm of freedom can only be based on the realm of necessity.

The error does not lie in continuing to see necessity, sacrifice and production in the new society. The error lies in consolidating these elements under the rubric of "labour time", reduced as much as possible, and universally opposing this to free time.

In "The Critique of the Gotha Program", Marx says that some day labour will constitute the most imperious human need. The Stalinists have constantly exploited this formula in a most odious manner. There is in any event a contradiction. Will labour in the communist society become a waste of time or a source of satisfaction? Is it therefore necessary to reduce labour time to a minimum, or should we, to the contrary, produce the maximum amount of labour possible to satisfy the demand for it? Only in capitalist society can labour appear as the most imperious need, as the only means to satisfy all the others. Only in capitalist society can it be both detested and demanded.

Fanciful

The whole idea of using labour time as a standard of measurement is somewhat fanciful.

The idea of measuring all productive activities by the time they require would be like measuring and comparing all liquids only by their volume. It is true that every activity takes a certain amount of time, just as a particular liquid occupies a certain volume. This is not a trivial point. A one-litre bottle of water could instead contain a litre of wine. But no one would ever deduce from that fact that a bottle of water is always equal to a bottle of wine, or alcohol, or soft drink, or hydrochloric acid. Strictly speaking, only from the narrow point of view of the wholesale dealer would this make sense.

Time is the only objective language that can be used to express the creative force of the slave or the worker, from the point of view of the exploiter. This implies external measurement, control and conflict. The duration and the intensity of the activity are privileged above its nature and its particular difficulty, which become matters of indifference. The subjectivity of what is experienced is sacrificed in favour of the objectivity of the standard of measurement. Creation and life are forced to submit to production and repetition.

Measuring by means of time is older than the commodity system. Instead of providing a certain quantity of a particular product, the exploited put a certain amount of their time at the disposal of the exploiter: the labour services of the feudal era, for example. This procedure was especially developed in the system of the Incas, a great agrarian empire under the unified rule of a bureaucracy where money was unknown. The labour services were performed in the form of days of labour spent in one or another task. This required a very rigorous system of accounting.

In the peasant or rural communities, an individual spent one day harvesting the fields of another person and vice-versa. The peasant and the blacksmith bartered their products on the basis of production time. The activity of a child was valued as a portion of that of an adult. These practices can be seen as the beginning of the use of time as universal standard and even of the submission of the planet to the commodity economy; but only the beginning. These marginal practices were more of the order of mutual aid than of exchange. The activities subject to measurement were of the same or concretely comparable nature. Measurement by time was not yet independent of the content of what was being measured.

With the dual development of the commodity system and the division of labour, measurement by means of time began to assume its fanciful character, becoming detached from the content of activity as the latter was diversified.

This process was accentuated when exchange penetrated into the sphere of production. Measurement by means of time developed in relation to the tendency of the economy to be based on labour time. The maximum amount must be produced in the least amount of time. The possibility to use time as a standard of measurement is inseparable from the compression of human activity within the smallest possible span of time. Not only did labour produce the commodity; the commodity produced labour through the despotism of the factory.

With this development, the practice of measurement by means of time lost its innocent airs, but was concealed behind money and justified by financial necessities.

Bourgeois ideologists, especially those who

invoke Saint Marx, project this fetishism of time and production over all of human history. In their view, the latter is nothing but an incessant struggle for free time. If primitive peoples remained primitive this is because, dominated by their low level of productivity, they did not have the time necessary for the accumulation of a surplus. Time is scarce; one must concentrate into it the densest activity possible.

Instead of thinking only about how to save time, primitive peoples were instead busy with the most effective means of squandering it. These peoples often present the most indolent character. Besides the tools needed for hunting, they hardly sought to accumulate goods of any kind.

In the 18th century, Adam Smith renounced the attempt to base value on labour time with reference to modern times. But this labour-value did play a role, according to Smith, in those primitive societies where things were still relatively uncomplicated.

Imagine, if you will, some hunters who want to exchange among themselves the various animals they took in the hunt. Upon what basis can they do this, other than the basis of labour time, as a function of the time required to get the animals? This is the assumption made by an economistic and banker's mentality when confronted by a situation where the rules of sharing and reciprocal bonds prevail.

Let us assume, however, that exchange already existed or that our primitive peoples decided to rationally employ their forces to acquire meat with the least expenditure of effort. Would they have constructed their system on the basis of necessary labour time?

There are pleasures and risks involved in hunting, concerning which the time employed in hunting is totally uninformative. What is the comparative value of a lion as opposed to an antelope, when considered on the basis of the duration of the hunt without reference to the different risks involved in each hunt? Certain modes of hunting may take more time but may also be more certain of success, less arduous, less dangerous, and more or less cruel.

If they still wanted to practice this type of measurement, could they do so? It is hard to evaluate with precision the time necessary to obtain this or that animal. By systematically hunting the most productive animals, from this narrow point of view, they would risk modifying the conditions and the necessary time for the hunt. In any event, one often goes out to hunt antelopes and comes home with rabbits. It is useless to predict the unpredictable.

Will we be told that this is no longer valid for our civilized epoch, and that the hunt is a very special case of productive activity? Let's face the facts. It is the ubiquity of exchange that conceals reality. Measurement by means of labour time does not exempt us from the hazards of human existence or of the exhaustion of natural resources. These problems are not specific to primitive man but apply to all societies. Not acknowledged by the logic of capital they return with a vengeance....

Measurement by time only indirectly accounts for any repercussions on the environment and the difficulty of the activity concerned. Can it be used in communism by translating the transformation or destruction of a rural region, the exhaustion of a mine's resources, or the production of oxygen in a forest, into its language? The inherent advantages or drawbacks of a production process will be reckoned in terms of the labour time that is virtually saved or virtually expended. It would surpass the absurdity of capitalism if it were to seek to consciously reduce use values and qualities to labour-values. What value does a stretch of countryside have? Should it be based on the expenditure that would be required to rebuild it from scratch? At this price, nothing would be worth undertaking.

To assess the different values of two labour processes of equal duration in which the risks or the discomfort of the jobs are different, do we have to find a single standard by which they can be compared? One hour of bricklaying would count as one and a half hours of carpentry. Let us say that the difference would be accounted for by the expenditure of time necessary to provide for the bricklayer, to wash his clothing ... and we refuse to reduce everything to the expenditure of labour time, but then how can we establish the coefficients that express the differences in value or discomfort that distinguish the two jobs? Why, on the other hand, should we want to establish such coefficients when these differences depend on the conditions and the rhythm of the activities concerned and the inclinations of the participants?

When the workers take over, the advocates of measurement by time or remuneration as a function of labour time run the risk of being left behind. From the moment when activity ceases to be compulsory, its nature will change and its duration will be extended. The quantity and the character of production will no longer be evaluated with respect to the duration of the consumed labour. One person will produce enough in a little time, while another will take a long time to produce little. If remuneration were to be based on the time expended then we will need to have strict prison guards on the jobsite or we would soon be faced with an incitement to laziness.

Whether the workers will agree to guarantee a certain amount of production or devote a certain number of hours each day to productive labour, is a question of practical organization that is not directly pertinent to the determination of the cost of what they produce. In one factory it might take twice as long as another factory to produce objects of the same cost.

One can certainly speak of the social allocation of labour time at the community's disposal, but one must not forget that time is not a material that one can dish out with a ladle. It will be men who will go to such and such a location in order to assume responsibility for such and such a task. From the moment when free time is no longer extraordinarily scarce and is not devoted to the satisfaction of absolutely vital needs, there will be some jobs that are more urgent than others, and men who work faster than other men.

With capital it is necessary to dissociate the price, the expenditure of labour power and what this expenditure contributes, and the labour that does not have any value. With communism this dissociation makes no sense. Labour power and labour, man and his activity, can no longer be separated.

This means, first of all, that there is no more surplus value, not even for the benefit of the community, or a new form of social surplus. One can no longer speak of accumulation or of expansion except in physical and material terms. To speak of socialist accumulation is an absurdity even if at any given moment more steel or more bananas are produced than before, even if more social time is devoted to production. These processes no longer assume the form of value or time employed.

As a result, this means that labour, which in capitalism has no value, acquires value in communism. This value that it acquires is neither moral nor monetary. This is not the apotheosis of labour but instead expresses its supersession.

Labour, the source of value, is not susceptible to numerical measurement. One can economize on it, but its identity is unquestionable. In communism this or that activity will no longer be distinguished from the effort made by the human beings who engage in it. Not all jobs have the same human cost. It is a matter of developing the least costly ones.

In capitalist society, if one shifts one's perspective from that of capital to that of the worker, labour also has a cost; one job is preferable to another. When night arrives one feels one's fatigue or anxiety. But finally the differences are small. Labour is always considered time that is more or less lost. No one devotes any time to calculating boredom or health damage. For the worker the price of all of this shit is his wage. One already knows that it is a mystification and that the wage is not determined by the effort expended or the discomfort experienced.

The superiority of communism lies in the fact that is not content with the satisfaction of the needs of "consumption". It applies its efforts to the transformation of productive activities, that is, to the conditions of labour. As a matter of principle, investment decisions will not be made on the basis of the economy of labour time, even if the possibility exists that the task can be expedited. These decisions will have the objective of producing the conditions in which activities can be enriched, favouring the most pleasant ones. The determination of the conditions of activity does not mean that the activity itself and the behaviour of the producers themselves will be determined in advance. The producer will still be master of his activity, but he will act in certain conditions, within the framework of certain limitations that constitute the arena in which he can act.

The production by men of the instruments and the plan of production allow for this transformation of human activity. The development of technology can be oriented so as to be more or less favourable for the producers. This or that kind of machine or ensemble of machines could allow those who use them to experience less exhaustion and be less subject to a certain rhythm of production. Those characteristics that would allow men to be as free as possible can be systematically developed in the productive process.

Don't tell us that personal preferences or subjectivity would objectively prevent any such choices. There are some things that do not change. We are not saying that the criteria must have a universal scope. They will vary according to the time and the situation. Men will make agreements to determine what suits them best. The diversity of personal preferences and the willingness to experiment can follow different roads in the context of a similar objective.

The estimation of costs cannot be reduced to the need to balance "income and expenditures"; equilibrium must be conceived as a dynamic equilibrium. Starting from the basis of the conditions inherited from capitalism, what is required is to give development a certain direction. Is the estimated cost of constructing a particular productive facility or way of life justified? Does the automation of this or that unit of production justify the efforts required for the fabrication of the automated machinery? The logic of the economy of labour time that serves as the organizing principle of the construction of situations in the capitalist world will yield to a different logic, a logic that is no longer external to the men that put it into practice. Humanity will organize and control the construction of situations in view of its needs. In this sense it will become situationist.

Elevator or Stairs?

Behind the economic idea of cost we once again find the most ordinary and banal reality, which that idea has ended up concealing.

Each person reflects on the question of whether what he is doing is worth the effort. Does the inevitable result justify the expense or the risk? Are there less costly, that is, more pleasant, ways to obtain an equivalent result or one that is good enough?

If such questions arise concerning the economy, they are only asked by economists or managers. In fact, economic and financial problems comprise a special, and rather strange, case of a more general problem.

The spontaneous and ingenuous evaluation of costs took place long before the advent of capitalism. It subsists at the margin of the economic sphere even though our choices must always take financial necessities into account. What characterizes this kind of evaluation is that it is effected without monetary subterfuges and is not reduced to temporal criteria.

Strictly speaking, the ability to evaluate costs is not a natural endowment peculiar to the human species. The pigeon that hesitates before pecking at the seeds you offer it is, in its own way, also evaluating costs. That he might make a mistake in his calculations and end up in the pot does not constitute a contradiction of this claim. Evaluation does not necessarily exclude the possibility of error.

The bird's choice depends more on instinct and habit than any other factor. With human beings we move to another level.

The individual who finds himself at the entrance to a building, and intends to go to an upper floor, and who has to choose between using the elevator and walking up the stairs, confronts a problem of evaluating costs. He might spend an hour reflecting on the problem or he might automatically make his decision without thinking about it.

The problem is simple if it is reduced to the three solutions that are obviously available: the elevator, the stairs, or cancelling his appointment in the building in question. It becomes more complicated if the elements that may or may not consciously intervene in the decision making process are taken into consideration. What floor does he have to go to? Does he know which one? Is he in good health? Is he elderly? Tired? Handicapped? How high are the steps? How steep is the stairway? How fast is the elevator and how often does it run? How urgent is his errand in this building?

The decision will not be an economic decision. It will be subjective, directly connected to a concrete situation. It is not a monetary decision. It does not involve an inquiry regarding which possible solution would be more expensive, since the elevator is free to use. The question of speed may play a role in his choice, it could prove to be decisive, but it is not necessarily connected with the situation. The economy of time would be given top priority if he were a fireman, if he did not prefer to use the ladder on his fire truck.

How can a procedure that is properly foreign to the economic sphere be applied to the economy? This is a false problem. The real problem is to go beyond the economy and to dissolve it as a separate sphere.

It is a question of doing away with the economy. This will not be achieved by suddenly discovering that we can replace today's methods with more direct and simpler procedures. Paradoxically, the development of the economy, the socialization of production, the generalized interdependence of enterprises, and the implementation of economic forecasting and calculation, make this rupture possible.

In the future, the principles that inform our choices will be as simple and as transparent as the ones we presently apply on a daily basis. They will be concerned with the reduction of effort, fatigue, and expenditures in general. These considerations will not in themselves constitute the goals of social life, but will comprise one aspect of the projects of the future depending on the nature of the latter. Perhaps very difficult and dangerous problems will have to be solved but we will have to try to address them. A team of mountain climbers can attempt to reach the summit of a difficult mountain, but this does not mean they have to do so with their bare hands.

Simple principles do not always entail easy methods and solutions. The degree of difficulty of an undertaking derives from the nature and the complexity of the problems that have to be solved. It could also be the result of the unsuitability of the methods of calculation applied to the object in question or a difficulty in determining the criteria of choice. The risk of error and the need to be satisfied with approximations by no means invalidate the procedure. In any event this would not constitute a step backwards with respect to current conditions.

What applies today to the use of the elevator or the stairs, will also apply tomorrow to their production and installation. The objective foundations of the individual's choices will no longer be economically determined.

Is it better to construct a stairway, an elevator, both, or nothing at all? These questions imply a whole series of subsidiary questions. Is it worth the effort to go to the upper floors? Is this requirement so important or so frequently necessitated that it justifies the necessary expense to build the stairway, the elevator, the rope or the kick in the ass that will get you to the desired floor? We can reverse the perspective. Given the cost of elevators should we construct such tall buildings? On the other hand, given the pleasures experienced by those who manufacture elevators, should we build more skyscrapers?

The list of questions that can be posed is practically endless. This may seem discouraging. In reality only a small number will be posed. Many will be ruled out by simple common sense. Our mountain climbers cannot demand an elevator for their expedition. Each decision will be made on the basis of a concrete situation in which a vast number of questions will already have been answered in advance by the facts themselves. Custom plays tricks on us, but it also spares us much trouble. It is quite likely that the man who is standing at the front door of the building will base his decision on habit. The evaluation of costs only acquires its full significance when one encounters a new situation, when a new productive process emerges. The problem of the fabrication and the installation of the elevator and the stairway could very well be a common problem that is solved according to known parameters. A special or unprecedented situation will be addressed as a modified form of a more classical situation.

There is a hierarchy of solutions. When the decision is made to build a house, the costs of the means to get to the upper floors will probably be of secondary importance. Once the more general decision is made, the builders will have to construct a stairway, an elevator, or both. The existing options will depend on the nature and the quality of the available materials. Choices can only be made in accordance with the products and the technologies that are currently in use and development within this sector. Every choice tends to miss the optimal solution, but every choice is made in accordance with a certain number of unavoidable objective conditions. The optimal solution may end up being a compromise between the interests of the different groups of people affected by the decision in question.

The end of the division of the economy into separate competing enterprises does not mean that all social production will assume the form of one big coordinated enterprise where every activity will be immediately subsumed to another, where there will be only one common interest and where the evaluation of costs will be undertaken directly on a worldwide scale. For human and technical reasons, the producers will be fragmented into separate groups whose interests will no longer be antagonistic, but whose opinions may very well be divergent. Since individuals may move from one job to another, from one workshop or construction site to another, and the membership of work crews may not be permanent, this fragmentation in time and space will persist.

The construction of a building implies the involvement of various skilled trades. We can imagine that in communism the architect will also be a labourer, a bricklayer or a painter. This will not obviate the fact that, especially if the construction project is very important, the workers will be divided into different teams and their tasks will be carried out at different stages of the project. The builders may be obliged to ask for outside help. They will have to get advice. They will have to obtain machinery and materials.

How will the cost of these products that come from outside the work unit be established and accounted for? The builders could attempt to facilitate the work where it is a question of the allocation and utilization of their own resources and capabilities. But when they have to avail themselves of warehoused goods that they did not themselves stock, such self-reliance is no longer possible. Certain materials that are easier to install, or that may have a reputation for providing more satisfaction to the users of the building, might nonetheless be rejected because of the cost of their manufacture. In every situation it is necessary for the advantages obtained to justify the expense incurred in order to avoid problems.

Products, and even production processes, must have an objectively determined cost. The users will make a rational choice on the basis of these costs.

Does this mean that each product will have a "price tag"? Will the housewife, when grocery shopping, find a bar code on her carrots and cabbages?

That would be an unfortunate recrudescence of today's society. As a general rule, each person will take what he needs when it is available and pay no attention to any other more urgent claim than his own. The calculation of costs is first of all in the nature of a forecast and its direct outcome is manifested in the nature and the quantity of the available goods. There is no need to put price labels on goods in order to put pressure on the intentions of the user, not to speak of his wallet.

There are various kinds of cement that presently have, and will continue to have, different costs of production. It would be stupid to use a kind of cement that is twice as expensive as another that would serve the same purpose. As a general rule, the nature of the product or its mode of employment is sufficient to determine its desired use; where there is a risk of confusing the different grades of products it will be enough to specify along with the mode of employment of the product the cost differences among the various products.

Today, dead labour weighs upon living labour, and the past weighs upon the present. In communism, the cost of a product is not the expression of a value that has to be realized, or of equipment that has to be amortized. This means that the cost of an object will not necessarily represent the expense required to produce it. It will not even be the average necessary expense required to produce all products of the same kind.

A product will have the cost that will reflect the cost of replacing it under the prevailing conditions. There will be no reason for a rise or fall in productivity to be translated into a difference between the cost of production and the cost of sale. This will apply immediately even to the objects that were manufactured previously. This variation could result in an expansion of the production in question if it becomes more worthwhile. Decisions to increase investment in a productive process will not be based on a surplus of profits.

There may be differences in cost in the production of the same product or of two similar products. This difference may result from the preservation of relatively antiquated production processes. Or they may be determined by natural conditions. Agricultural output is quite variable, and not every mine is as easily exploited as another. Does this mean that similar products will have different costs, or that there will be an average cost that will be the same for all of them, just like today's average market price?

It will be very important for the differences in costs to be known. But this will not affect the users of the products in question. There will be no advantages for some and disadvantages for others; it will simply be a matter of developing the most advantageous production processes.

If the increase of the cost of production of a product implies a decrease in its cost-effectiveness, this does not mean that it must be rejected. First of all, its decrease in cost-effectiveness may be a temporary or periodic phenomenon; also, because one must evaluate the importance of the needs that have to be satisfied. Thus, with regard to food production, a rise in the cost of production often signifies a decreasing crop yield. Let us assume that less fertile soils are cultivated. This would be no reason to refuse to feed part of the population and instead shift the resources in question to more cost-effective activities.

Decreasing yields could on the other hand be a short-term phenomenon. Sowing crops in a desert is not very promising; but major investments, such as irrigation projects and new methods of farming, could make a big difference. A sun-baked desert, once it is watered, or a fish farm, could be more productive than traditionally fertile soils.

What seems to be impossible today will be

possible tomorrow. Modern technologies, instead of furthering the arms race, will be used to make the deserts bloom.

From the moment when there is a rising demand for a good, there is a risk that this could lead to a fall or a rise in the production cost incurred by the new production units. A fall in the production cost will have a tendency to increase the demand for the product. If on the other hand there is a rise in the production cost of a product, then we will have to know when the cost becomes prohibitive. In this case it must be determined if it is the recent increase in demand that must be curtailed or whether, to the contrary, this demand must be satisfied by abandoning or reducing the demand for other products.

Calculation

In communism, just as in capitalism, in order to estimate costs and to select the optimal solutions, comparisons must be made. How are we to compare?

As long as there is money, that is, a universal equivalent, everything is simple since any good can be evaluated in accordance with this single standard. There is a quantitative relation between

all products. When, however, we decide to do
without money and even without measurement by
the quantity of labour, on what basis can we make
comparisons? What else do all goods have in
common that makes them comparable?

There is no other single and universally valid
standard. We shall therefore have to do without
one. But this will not prevent comparisons from being
made. These comparisons will be qualitative and
will be based on different and variable standards.
They will no longer be carried out in accordance
with an abstract and universal reference, but will be
connected to concrete situations and goals.

What is bizarre is the fact that different goods
can be equal to each other regardless of their
specific natures. It is understandable for foods to be
compared in accordance with their protein content
or their freshness. But these distinct criteria do not
allow for the definition of a general standard of
equivalence.

The need for a general standard of equivalence
cannot be dissociated from the need to engage in
exchange. All things must be capable of being
subjected to comparison from a universal point of
view because they have become exchangeable
goods and economic values. This is precisely what
must disappear and this is what the dream—or the

nightmare—of measurement by means of labour time seeks to preserve by giving it a new disguise.

Even under the rule of capital, not all comparisons can be reduced to comparisons of value. Goods still have use values. The buyer's evaluation is made not only with reference to price, but also with reference to the usefulness and the quality of the product.

When a housewife goes shopping and chooses between a lettuce and a bunch of radishes she does so according to the taste of her son, the meal of the day, the appearance of the product, how much room she has in her basket.... Price is not really determinate except when two identical products have different values.

The multiplicity of criteria that come into play does not prevent this person from making his comparisons and his choice. His criterion is subjective. It is not universally valid. This does not mean that it is irrational with respect to the situation in question.

When the situation involves choosing between various manufacturing procedures it will be necessary to find a more general basis for comparison. The choice will be less subjective in the sense that it must not depend on a passing whim, because it will have long-term repercussions.

Under current conditions it is sometimes the case that purely monetary evaluations are not decisive or are modified by other considerations. The risk posed by major swings in certain prices over the course of time or political requirements prevent automatic compliance with the strictly financial viewpoint.

Let us consider the question of nuclear power. In opposition to economic arguments in its favour, questions have been raised that focus on the environmental, social and political costs of nuclear power. The debate is often carried on with a degree of bad faith, about energy yields, problems of transport and storage of wastes, of national sovereignty, and the creation or elimination of jobs.

In communist society it is no longer necessary to make all comparisons on a universal scale. It suffices to be able to determine the possibilities that really exist and to favour those that offer the most rapid results, those that will be the safest, the least dangerous....

What is essential is to determine a set of pertinent criteria and in accordance with these criteria to directly address the diverse solutions that can be discerned. It is not so much a matter of quantifying as it is of ordering the various criteria and solutions. What predominates is the relative, qualitative meaning.

We are not saying we will rely on computers to arrange everything but they will be necessary and useful.

"Conceived at first for accounting operations and later used for management, as well as being used for scientific calculations, they were long considered (for perhaps ten years...) as instruments for generating quantitative results. This has changed. Thanks to the methods of cybernetics, and especially to those of simulation, the accumulation of numbers led to a qualitative result: what is of interest is no longer the exact numbers but their meaning relative to which a choice is made. In this way, calculating machines have become means for management forecasting."

– Robert Faure, Jean-Paul Boss and Andre Le Garff, 'La recherché operationnelle', Presses universitaires de France, Paris (Vendôme, Impr. des P.U.F.), 1961

What must be simplified and universalized is not so much the factors of decision that come into play as the procedures of decision making, the programs that allow one to address a mass of data.

In a certain sense, the more important the criteria, the more accurate the representation of reality.

We could imagine the general contours of a future debate on the importance of various energy sources. A vast amount of data will come into play. A single criterion can only be used at the cost of distorting reality. Comprehensive decisions will have to be made in accordance with the different resources and needs of each region.

Communism does not rule out purely quantitative comparisons and decisions. They will still be valid when a single criterion of selection is sufficient, according to the nature of the products under consideration. This would be the case when it is a matter of increasing or decreasing the output of a particular production process. It would also prevail when the savings of expenditure corresponds to a qualitative savings in the utilization of a raw material devoted to the same use, as in the case of canned food. But even in this case, the savings must not be considered as a savings in labour time, but simply in the quantity of raw materials. That this decision could result in a reduction in the time spent in productive activity is simply one possible outcome.

Shouldn't we fear this communist frenzy of rationalization? Does it not run the risk of becoming similar to the capitalist frenzy of exploitation?

Today, rationalization and exploitation are conflated. Man tends to be considered as an object from which you try to get as much as possible. Inhuman methods have been developed that do not derive from technical requirements: hellish work rhythms, working two or three shifts. Capitalist rationalization, whether brutal or subtle, is always carried out to a greater or lesser degree to the detriment of men. It is always irrational.

Communist rationalization does not have the goal of imposing a rhythm of work. Its essential tendency will be to increase the freedom and pleasure of humans. Decision-making and the implementation of decisions will not be carried out without regard for the preferences and the customs of those affected. There will still be technical requirements and production necessities that will influence the course and duration of human activity. But this will have nothing to do with making human capital profitable.

6. Beyond Politics

Communism is not a political movement. It is the critique of the State and of politics.

The intention of the revolutionaries is not to conquer and wield state power, even if it were for the purpose of destroying it. The party of communism does not take the form of a political party and has no intention of competing with organizations of that kind.

With the establishment of the communist community all political activity as a distinct activity oriented towards the acquisition of power for the sake of power will disappear. There will no longer be, on the one hand, the economic—the sphere of necessity, and on the other hand, the political—the sphere of freedom.

The End of the State

The cult of the state is fundamentally anti-communist.

This cult is paradoxically spawned from and reinforced by all the shortcomings, all the weaknesses, and all the conflicts that are engendered by capitalist society. It is the supreme saviour; the last resort of widows and orphans. Incidentally, and although it pretends to be above all classes and presents itself as the guarantor of the general interest against the excesses of individuals and groups, it is devoted to the defence of property and privilege.

There was a time when the rising bourgeoisie

exhibited anti-state sentiments. Today the most that it exhibits with regard to the state is annoyance. The era when bourgeois revolutionaries claimed that the happiest peoples were peoples without a state is far behind us. The increasing threat posed by the proletariat, the rise of competing imperial powers, and the scale of economic crises have demonstrated the value of possessing a powerful state machine that is primarily a good repressive apparatus.

The political parties fight among themselves to conquer, in the name of the people, this state machine that is presented as a neutral instrument. Consistent Leninists proclaim the class nature of the state and the impossibility of controlling it through a simple electoral victory. They conclude from this the need to dismantle it, but only in order to replace it with a "workers' state".

It was to the honour of the anarchists to have maintained a fundamental anti-statism.

However, even more than with respect to money, the whole world believes in the duty of heaping abuse on the state. Everyone complains about the stupidity of its administration, the high taxes, the arrogance of the police, the venality of the politicians, the ignorance of the voters.... But what apparently lies beyond the pale of their imagination is the prospect of the State's disappearance. And this is what they get: power without imagination.

The state has intervened ever more openly in social life over the last few decades. The rise of Stalinism and fascism signified merely a few more flagrant steps in this direction. Where some have believed they could see the state becoming a people's state, it is necessary to see instead the accentuation of the control of the state over its population.

Of particular importance in this regard is the usurpation or the integration into the state apparatus of the organizations of workers' defence and solidarity. Through various channels such as social welfare measures, the trade union apparatuses have been subjected to the state. This has allowed them to act more or less like political special interest groups. We must not be deceived by their declarations of independence and opposition, since they are just performing their assigned roles.

This integration of the struggle and this bureaucratization of social groups have obviously been presented as great victories of the working class. The workers' struggles benefit a layer of specialists in contestation and result in an increasing institutionalization of the "workers'" organizations. Often, these "victories" do not result in even a redistribution of resources towards the most disadvantaged layers but instead just end up costing them more money. This is true regardless of the hypocritical claims of the trade unions and state officials.

Increasing state control must not be considered solely as a factor weakening the proletariat. It corresponds, to the contrary, to the need to control the proletariat's increasing power. This increasing state control compensates for the fragility of modern societies; but it is not itself exempt from this fragility. The statist regimentation of the population is only possible thanks to the complicity of the population. The anti-political revolution will reveal the utterly superficial nature of this regimentation.

Unlike politicians of every stripe, revolutionaries are very careful not to appeal to the responsibility of the state when a problem arises. They systematically assert, first of all, the autonomy and the self-organization of the proletarian class. Invoking the weakness of the proletariat in order to justify reliance on the state is to justify and confirm this weakness as eternal.

Revolutionary society will have institutions of coordination and centralization. It will in many cases allow for a higher degree of worldwide centralization than is currently allowed by capital. But it will not need a state in which power will be concentrated, that whole machinery of repression, identification, control and education. In revolutionary society the administration of things will replace the government over men.

The problem lies in the need to avoid recreating some kind of state in an insurrectionary or transitional stage, while nonetheless ensuring that administrative and repressive, and therefore typically state, functions, are carried out. Those who do not want to face this problem, like the anarchists, will only succeed in being crushed by the statists or will be obliged to become statists themselves. The participation of anarchist ministers in the Government Junta during the Spanish revolution illustrates just what can happen to those who persist in this attitude.

The solution to this problem, to this contradiction, has been outlined by proletarian insurrections since the Paris Commune. It is the workers' council, the councilist organization of social life.

The Workers' Councils

The Paris Commune already provided an initial glimpse of what a workers' government would look like.

In 1905, insurgent Russian workers elaborated the form of the soviet. This institution formed by factory delegates was at first devoted to the coordination of the struggle. It was gradually transformed into an administrative institution whose purpose was to replace the official governing bodies of the state. Even part of the police force passed under the control of the Petrograd Soviet. Its existence came to an end with the arrest of its deputies by Czarist forces.

The same thing happened again in 1917, but this time with more extensive participation on the part of the military. The Bolshevik coup d'état in October 1917 was carried out in the name of transferring all power to the soviets. Its basis of support was the soviets, where the Bolsheviks controlled the military committees and had obtained majorities in the Petrograd and Moscow soviets. This victory was the beginning of the end for the soviets. With the reflux of the revolution, the onset of civil war, and the reinforcement of the power of the Bolshevik party and its administrative apparatus, the soviets were gradually deprived of their original content. The last show of resistance to this process, offered by the Kronstadt naval base, was crushed in 1921 by the Red Army led by Trotsky, the former president of the Petrograd soviet.

The proletarian revolutions of the 20th century have repeatedly led to the re-emergence of the soviet form. In the immediate aftermath of World War One and the Russian Revolution, workers' councils were formed in Hungary, Germany and Italy. During the Spanish war, workers and peasants committees arose throughout the country. In Hungary, in 1956, factory delegates formed the Workers' Council of Greater Budapest. In Poland, in 1971, the insurgent workers of the Baltic ports once again utilized this form of organization.

The word "council" actually embraces quite diverse organizational forms, even if we exclude those institutions of co-management or workers' management that have nothing revolutionary about them. They range from the factory or neighbourhood committee to the soviet that administers a big city or even a region. It is incorrect to seek to distinguish among these organizations in order to confer the title of "workers' council" only on some of them.

We do not advocate one or another variety of council. We advocate the council organization of society. This implies and requires different levels of organization that complement and sustain one another. What would be unfortunate, and this is what has regularly taken place, would be if one of these levels should be predominant.

For example, the factory committee could be reduced to the exercise of a simple function of workers' control or strictly limited to managing one productive unit. The absence of real soviets in Spain and Catalonia, despite the flourishing base committees, left the field open to the republican state and the politicians; hence the anarchist dilemma.

The soviet, on the other hand, if it were to be separated from its base, could become a kind of regional state or workers' parliament. In this case it would cease to be an active anti-political institution and would instead become a battleground for competing political parties.

What gives the workers' council its revolutionary character and its anti-political content is principally the fact that it arises directly from the masses in action. It is composed of a pyramid of committees that give rise to one another, but without the apex of the pyramid ever being able to conceive of itself as independent of the base of the pyramid.

The committees are not simple voting assemblies that delegate power among themselves from the bottom upward. Each level carries out practical functions. Each committee is an active community. It delegates to a higher-level committee those problems which it cannot solve itself. It does not thereby abdicate its sovereignty. All delegates must explain their actions and are responsible to the base and revocable at any time.

The workers' council does not reproduce within its structure the division between the legislative, executive and judicial powers. It endeavours to unify and concentrate these functions in its hands. Even if it lays down rules it acts, above all, in accordance with the situation, without hiding behind an arsenal of formal laws.

The workers' council constitutes itself as a tribunal to adjudicate conflicts; to judge, to resolve, and to punish. These actions are carried out with reference to each concrete situation. What is subject to judgment is not the seriousness of the transgression, but the objective risks and dangers for the revolution and for society.

The legitimacy of the council is not based upon a few democratic elections that would make it a consecrated vessel of the people's will. It is not the representative of the masses. It "is" the organized masses. The individuals and groups that assume responsibility for particular tasks are not necessarily elected. But when they commit themselves to act on behalf of the entire council they are responsible to its general assemblies. The council does not claim to be the general expression of all of society, or to be located above all the conflicts that affect the latter.

It is an institution of the class and of the struggle. This implies that there must be a certain amount of agreement within its ranks. It cannot tolerate divergences of opinion that would paralyze it.

The workers' council can be viewed as an ultra-dictatorial or as an ultra-democratic institution. It is both and yet neither. It is ultra-dictatorial in the sense that it is only answerable to itself and insofar as it casts the principles of the division of powers to the winds. It is ultra-democratic in the sense that it allows for a degree of debate and participation by the masses that was never achieved by the most democratic state.

Above all, the workers' council is not a political institution, since it no longer separates the citizen from the social individual. In this respect it transcends both dictatorship and democracy, which are the two faces of politics, even if it makes use of forms or procedures that are democratic or dictatorial.

The council is neither the instrument of a popular democracy, nor the instrument of the dictatorship of the proletariat. These expressions are not suitable for describing the phase that comprehends the break between capitalism and communism.

The workers' councils of the past, with the exception of a few rare instances, never rose to the level of the program that we are sketching here.

They were managerial, bureaucratic, indecisive, dispute-ridden, and incapable of attaining a perspective that was in accord with their own nature. They were destroyed. This does not prove that the council form does not work, but rather that it was assayed on a terrain that was still unfavourable for its development.

In 1956, the Workers' Council of Greater Budapest, which then administered an entire region of Hungary, proclaimed its own suicide with its call for the reestablishment of parliamentary democracy.

Previously, the workers' councils at least had the merit of having existed. They demonstrated the workers ability to run their own affairs, and to take factories and cities into their hands. They were connected with formidable movements by means of which the workers overthrew, at least temporarily, bourgeoisie and bureaucrats. If these experiences have been dissimulated and distorted this is because the prospect of the proletariat picking up where it left off in Catalonia, Poland and China is undesirable to some people: to dispense with masters and to proceed from there.

The counterrevolution, even in the Soviet Union, has never been able to coexist with councils. The fact that the councils have demonstrated their moderation is one thing. It is another thing entirely for the counterrevolution to show moderation in regard to the councils.

The best expressions of the workers' councils were provided when they had to respond quickly, unambiguously and with a strong hand to their enemies. They were forged directly as an organization of struggle. Their program may have been limited but they were aware of this.

On other occasions they became entangled in administrative details and procrastination. At these times their only reason for existence seemed to be the absence of bourgeois power. They elaborated magnificent organizational plans. But this was carried out in a vacuum, removed from the imperatives of struggle. The apparent absence of danger led to the worst illusions.

In such cases, the council appeared to be more of a working class response to the vacuum left by the bourgeoisie than an organizational form imposed by the radical demands of the struggle itself.

We support workers' councils but we are not in favour of the councilist ideology. This ideology does not perceive the councils as a moment of the revolution, but as the goal of the revolution. For the councilist ideology, socialism is the replacement of the power of the bourgeoisie by the power of the councils, and capitalist management by workers' management; from this perspective the success or failure of the revolution is an organizational question. Where the Leninists make everything depend on the party, the councilists make everything depend on the council.

The workers' councils will be what they make of themselves. The only way they can be victorious is to undertake and to embody the organization of communization.

For communists, the revolution is not a question of organization. What determines the possibility of communism is a certain level of development of the productive forces and the proletarian class. There are problems of organization, but they cannot be addressed independently of what it is that is being organized, of the tasks that are faced. Are we saying that the rules of organization are neutral, or that they are purely technical questions? Of course not. Such choices are of great importance. Some organizational rules are adapted and conducive to communist action. Others hinder it. But it is a serious illusion to believe that the implementation of certain rules, especially regarding the control of delegates, is sufficient to avoid bureaucratization, deception and schism. Bureaucrats are professionals of organization as a separate organization. They like to stress the preliminaries to action rather than action itself. Detailed and unsuitable rules, even if they are formally anti-bureaucratic, run the risk of actually facilitating bureaucratization.

However slight the progress of the councils, when they cannot be easily liquidated, the worst enemies of the revolution will claim to be councilists in order to more easily put an end to them. They will try to transform them into the private preserve of their manoeuvres, and to exclude the real revolutionaries from the councils.

Can we conclude, on the basis of the fact that the councils of the past often had little that was communist about them, that their time has passed, and that all institutionalization is counterrevolutionary?

We do not see the workers' council as just one more institution. The revolution, whether we like it or not, will encounter problems of administration, the preservation of order, and the unification of opposed tendencies. It will be necessary to govern, if not men, then at least some men. One could very well maintain that looting is a healthy reaction to the provocation of commodity society and poverty. It could play a beneficial role in the phase of rupture, with the rout and downfall of the commodity. But looting cannot be institutionalized; it cannot be the normal mode of communist distribution of products.

It is impossible to allow all products to be subject to free distribution. It will be necessary to organize, allocate, and restrict. This is the task of the councils.

As the scarcity of goods is diminished and the power of the counterrevolution declines, the councils will lose their statist character. They will not be abolished. They will have deep roots in the life of society.

To reject the councils due to purism is, from the moment when they arise to meet real needs, to situate oneself outside the revolutionary process. It would be better to participate in their creation, their operation and their eventual dissolution in accordance with the struggle and the correlation of forces between revolution and counterrevolution.

Participation in the councils does not mean that revolutionaries must renounce their own autonomous action and organization. The councils are mass organizations. Hence they will exhibit a certain degree of hesitation, and a slower rate of radicalization than certain fractions of the population. The development of the councils will to some degree be determined by what is done by those organized outside them.

It will be necessary to fight and to boycott the corporatist councils, the managerial organizations, the neo-trade unionist or neo-political groups that will seek to seize the organization of social life for the benefit of a minority. Organizations that will maintain commodity production, form police units, or demand the return of the capitalists, cannot be considered to be soviets....

The council is necessary when a territory has to be administered. It disappears when this necessity temporarily ceases to exist as a result of a certain relation of forces or permanently ceases to exist as a result of the consolidation of communism. Certain groups can, in accordance with a revolutionary situation, intervene and communize stocks of commodities without being capable of or wanting to take the production or distribution of these commodities in their hands on a more permanent basis. It all depends on when the revolutionary forces reckon they possess the means to advance from specific wildcat actions to the direct administration of a region. The advantage of taking such a step would be an improved position with regard to securing resources for feeding the population or waging the revolutionary war. The disadvantage would be that the liberated region would become a target for attack. From the moment that this risk is accepted the problem of the councilist organization of the liberated region is posed: the problem of the constitution of a revolutionary power.

This same power! Whilst it must attempt to acquire the broadest support and participation of the masses, should not accept formal democracy as its basis, by organizing elections, for example.

Democracy

What on Earth could be more beautiful than democracy, the power of the sovereign people? As the word "capitalism" assumes more pejorative connotations, "democracy" gains adherents. The whole world is for democracy, whether constitutional monarchy or republic, bourgeois or people's democracy. If there is one thing everyone accuses their enemies of, it is that they are not democratic enough.

Anyone who criticizes democracy can only be, in the best case, a nostalgic apologist for the old absolute monarchies. Generally the appalling label of "fascist" is the preferred epithet reserved for such people. The most fanatic mudslingers in this regard are often the Marxists and Marxist-Leninists who forget what the founding fathers said about democracy, and who praise democracy so much in order to conceal their own taste for power and dictatorship... Ironically enough, it is certain elements tainted with the brush of Stalinism that will hypocritically accuse us of being Stalinists.

Democracy seems to be the antithesis of capitalist despotism. Where everyone knows that it is a minority that really rules, it is common for people to set against this minority rule the power derived from universal suffrage.

In reality, capitalism and democracy go hand in hand. Democracy is the fig leaf of capital. Democratic values, far from being subversive, are the idealized expression of the really existing and somewhat less than noble tendencies of capitalist society. Communists are no more eager to realize the trinity of "liberty, equality, fraternity" than that of "work, family, fatherland".

If democracy is the consort of capital, why do dictatorship and capitalism so often coexist? Why do most people live under authoritarian regimes? Why is it that, even in democratic states, democratic functions are constantly impeded?

Democratic aspirations and values result from capitalism's tendency to act as a solvent in society. They correspond to the end of the era when the individual had his place in a stable community and network of relations. They also correspond to the need to preserve the image of an idealized community, to regulate conflicts, and to reduce friction for the good of the whole community. The minority yields to the will of the majority.

Democracy is not merely a lie or a vulgar illusion. It derives its content from a shattered social reality, which it seems to reunite into a totality. The democratic aspiration conceals a search for community and respect for others. But the soil in which it is rooted and attempts to grow prevents it from successfully attaining these goals.

Even so, democracy frequently poses too great a threat to capital or at least to certain powerful interests. This is why it is always encountering impediments to its existence. With few exceptions, these constraints and even unadorned dictatorship are presented as victories for democracy. What tyrant does not pretend to rule, if not through the people, at least for the people?

Democracy, which during calm periods can appear to be a useful means to pacify workers' struggles, is shamelessly abandoned when this is required for the defence of capital. There are always intellectuals and politicians who are very surprised when they are so easily sacrificed on the altar of the interests of the powerful.

Democracy and dictatorship are two contrasting, but not totally unrelated, forms. Democracy, since it implies the submission of the minority to the majority, is a form of dictatorship.

A dictatorial junta may very well have recourse, in order to make decisions, to democratic mechanisms.

It is often forgotten that fascism, Nazism and Stalinism have shared a predilection to impose both terroristic procedures and periodic elections. It is characteristic of them to oppose the masses of the population and their popular tribunes, on the one hand, to a handful of "traitors" and "unpatriotic" and "anti-party" individuals, on the other.

Communism is not the enemy of democracy because it is the friend of dictatorship and fascism. It is the enemy of democracy because it is the enemy of politics. Nonetheless, communists are not indifferent to the regime under which they live. They prefer to quietly go to bed each night without having to ask themselves if that will be the night when they will be dragged out of bed and taken to prison.

Critique of the state must not replace the critique of politics. Some attack the machinery of the state only in order to save politics. Just as some educational theorists criticize the school in order to generalize the educational paradigm to cover all forms of social relations, for the Leninists everything is political. Behind every manifestation of capital they see intention or design. Capital is thus transformed into the instrument of a political program that must be opposed by another political program.

Politics is supposed to be the terrain of liberty, of action and of movement, in contrast with the fatalism of economics. The economy, the domain of goods production, is ruled by necessity. Economic development and its crises appear to be natural phenomena that are beyond man's control.

The left has the habit of emphasizing the possibilities of politics, while the right focuses on economic necessities: this is a false debate.

Politics is increasingly prone to become a carbon copy of economic life. During a certain period it was capable of playing a role in the establishment of compromises and alliances between social layers.

Today, the significance of politics as a factor of economic intervention has grown. At the same time, however, the political sphere has lost its independence. There is nothing left of politics but a single political program of capital, which both the right and the left are forced to implement regardless of the specific interests of their respective constituencies.

While the state appears to be an institution with more or less recognizable boundaries, politics is constantly exuded from every pore of society. Even if it is manifested in the action of a particular milieu of militants or politicians, it relies upon and is echoed by the behaviour of every individual. This is what gives it its force and lays the foundation for the widespread opinion that the solution of any social problem can only be political.

Politics derives from the dissociation between decision-making and action, and on the separations which set individuals against one another. Politics appears first of all as a permanent quest for power that motivates men in capitalist society. Democracy and despotism seem to be the only forms for regulating problems that arise between people. The introduction of democracy into romantic relationships and families passes for a new stage in human progress. It expresses, in the first place and perhaps in the least unacceptable way, the loss of the profound unity that could exist between human beings.

Communism does not separate decision and execution. There will no longer be a separation between two groups or even between two distinct and hierarchical moments. People will do what needs to be done or what they have decided to do without considering whether or not the majority approves. Thoughts about majority vs. minority presuppose the existence of a formal community.

The principle of unanimity rules in the sense

that those who do something have reached an agreement in principle and this agreement has provided them with the basis and the possibility for common action. The group does not exist independently of, or prior to, the action. It is not split by a vote only to immediately be reunified by virtue of the submission of one part to the other. It is constituted in and through action, and by the ability of each individual to identify with and to understand the point of view of others.

It is not a matter of categorically rejecting all voting and all majority rule. These are technical forms which cannot be given an absolute value. It could happen that the minority is right. It could happen that the majority may yield to the minority in view of the importance of the question for the minority.

Is communism the advent of freedom? Yes, if by freedom you understand that men will have more possibilities for choice than they do now, and that they will be able to live in accordance with their inclinations.

What we reject is the philosophy that opposes free will and determinism. This separation reflects the opposition between man and the world, and between the individual and society. It is an expression of the anomie of the individual and his inability to understand his own needs in order to satisfy them. He can choose between a thousand jobs, a thousand kinds of leisure, and a thousand lovers, and will be influenced in a thousand ways, because nothing really concerns him. No certainty affects him. He doubts everything, starting with himself. As a result he is ready to put up with anything and often believes that he has made a choice. Freedom is presented as the philosophical garb of misery and doubt as the expression of freedom of opinion when it actually means wandering aimlessly, man's inability to find himself at home in the world.

During the course of the revolution man loses his chains but, having become his own objective, he is simultaneously chained to his desires and the needs of the moment. He becomes passionate and begins to know himself. The extraordinary climate of joy and tension of the insurrections is linked with the feeling that everything is possible and that what is being done must absolutely be brought to a conclusion as soon as possible. There is no longer any reason for doubt and for staggering from one meaningless task to another. Subjective and objective forces merge.

The Electoral Circus

If you confuse elections with democracy, we shall be told by subtle thinkers, this is because you know that you will lose.

We have no illusions. It is certain that, as long as the system is functioning normally, we would be utterly defeated in a general vote. Our program might not be considered to be entirely without its good points by the majority of the voters, but it would certainly be judged to be unattainable. Only by refusing to act as voters will it be possible for them to begin to perceive the possibility of its attainment.

If politics is the art of the possible, as they say, then we situate ourselves beyond the realm of that possibility.

Good upstanding democratic trendsetters and opinion leaders, are you willing to submit certain questions to the population and to abide by its wishes? Lackeys of capital, we ask you: are you prepared to hold a referendum to discover whether or not capitalism should be maintained? There is a multitude of questions that you have managed to prevent from ever being addressed. They are ruled out from the start as not realistic. You are the ones who determine what is and what is not possible. But that is not enough for you. It is also necessary for your realistic programs and predictions to have never been implemented.

The state exists thanks to the taxes paid by its citizens. Its rule is based on their votes. If each one of its policies had to be directly examined and approved on an item-by-item basis by the taxpayers, it would risk losing many of its supporters. When he pays, the citizen has the impression of having been screwed. When he votes, even if he knows better he knows that he cannot do anything but keep his mouth shut, and feels flattered that his opinion should be solicited.

There is a dissociation between the system's real management and the layers of officials who staff it on the one hand, and on the other, the politics of the parties, the spectacle-politics.

Electoral democracy serves to conceal the fact that all important decisions are beyond the control of the voters and even of the politicians.

The reality of electoral politics is becoming increasingly permeated by the commodity. Democracy appears as the direct reflection of the economic world. The voter is no longer even a citizen, but a consumer of programs and ideologies. The spectacle of politics and its privileged moments, known as elections, must be denounced for what it really is: just another way of making the people forget their nullity.

It often happens that the people take the hoax seriously. In the aftermath of an election that was annulled or after winning what seemed to them to be an electoral victory, they begin a rebellion. At this point they have gone beyond the reality of electoral politics.

We do not advocate participation in elections, let alone strict abstention. When the proletarians vote, even if they are not right, at least they have their reasons. This ritual will not seem to be really illusory, ridiculous and unfortunate until living conditions in their totality begin to really change. In the meantime voting will have its place in the armoury of the system.

Elections could very well be held in a communist organization. They will be for the purpose of designating delegates. But this election no longer has the appearance of a privileged moment. The designee does not have a blank check. He fulfils one function among others, one that is no more sacred than any other. Naming such a person or such a team of people, or approving of their previous activity, the rank and file is only establishing its own safeguards to ensure the implementation of its program. It is not the electoral procedure itself but the action that is undertaken that matters.

The formation of workers' councils is not

predicated on holding a referendum. Their task is not to liberate a region in order to hold elections there that would only be considered as valid by their organizers, as usual. With reference to this question we have the bad example of the Paris Commune.

Even if elections could be successfully conducted under these conditions, this would only succeed in dissociating decision-making and action and bringing about the return of professionals of politics. To have elections, voters must be registered and records must be kept.

The establishment of an administrative apparatus by means of elections presupposes the existence of such an apparatus! Power and the state were not born from elections, but the reverse.

The revolutionary organizations of the masses will be formed and consolidated in accordance with certain practical tasks. They will be born from the actions of minorities. You will not see 51% of the population suddenly take action, all at the same time, for the same purpose. These active minorities will be distinguished by the fact that they will not organize the rest of the population, but will tend to merge with the latter in attempts to resolve collective problems. Its success will depend on its ability to attract the participation of much more than just 51% of the population.

Communism cannot be established by means of a coup. Because it must confront the power of the state and its repressive apparatus, communism can only be victorious if it obtains the more or less active participation of a large part of the population, in which case its enemies would be an insignificant minority.

The proletarian revolution, by breaking the chains of the wage system, will make possible and necessary a degree of mass participation that cannot possibly be compared with that of the bourgeois political revolutions, even in those cases when the latter were popular revolutions. These popular revolutions, which the democrats invoke in their own favour, did not take place as a result of democratic deliberations. If the French people were given the choice in 1789, would they have voted for revolution? What actually took place was the result of one fraction of the population revolting against the superannuated privileges of the nobility. Driven forward by its successes and the consequences of its actions, the revolution swept away the worm-eaten system.

The party of communism will not follow behind the overwhelming majority of the population until the latter perceives communism as the direct means of resolving the problems of everyday life. The revolution does not take place because enough people have been converted to revolutionary views. People become revolutionary because the revolution causes a new way of life to appear, and it seems to them possible and necessary to live that way.

Today, when society's vaults are still full, the disappearance of money seems impossible. Those who advocate it come off as naïve dreamers. When the market mechanisms cease to function, however, to continue to depend on money for one's necessities will take on the aspect of meaningless acrobatics. People will come to support communism, not through ideology or even because of their loathing for a dying society, but due to a simple need to live. It will then become necessary to defend communism from the opportunists who are incapable of conceiving of a long-term perspective, and who will seek to gain immediate personal advantages from this situation.

If we say that the revolution must be based upon the broadest participation possible, why don't we proclaim our allegiance to democracy? This might pose a quandary for some of our opponents and perhaps even to some of our friends. But we are not, after all, politicians; superficial support is more hindrance than help. We need to be clear in order to unite and orient our supporters on a solid foundation. As for our genuine enemies, we do not want to make their jobs easier for them, but in any event what we really say or want makes little difference to them. Sometimes this is because they do not understand us, or because they want to slander us, except when they lift some ideas from the revolutionaries to spice up their program.

Democracy is supposed to be the power of the people, the power of all. The communist revolution does not expect to change the form of the power structure or to hand it over to the people. It wants to remove it from the entire world.

Power always needs external legitimization: God for the monarchy, the people for the constitutional monarchy or the republic. Are the people more real than God? No, God is a person, a representation full of humanity, while the people are nothing but a pure abstraction of humanity. This people that is invoked to legitimize the state is nothing but a reflection of the state. Between this ideal people, this political people, and the real, diverse, lively, stupid or intelligent people, the people revealed in everyday life, an abyss yawns.

It is not politics that expresses and embodies the ideas and the will of humans, but the latter become the vehicles for political opinions. They are themselves transformed into abstractions when, whether voters or militants, they express their opinions.

Why don't the communists, who want to do away with exploitation and war, renounce the use of force and dictatorial methods?

Do you really believe that the ruling classes will renounce the use of such means? Do you think that in a period of social transformation the most democratic states will not dictate their beautiful principles at gunpoint? The capitalists, the privileged, and the servants of the most liberal political order might claim they are fighting for democracy. They will not openly try to defend their real interests before the public. But it is quite unlikely that they will fight democratically.

It is within a context of a crisis situation that we have to compare bourgeois methods with revolutionary methods. It is hypocritical to contrast the behaviour of the most democratic bourgeois states during times of social peace with the behaviour of revolutionaries during a period of social conflict. In all likelihood the revolutionaries will prove to be more human and more democratic than the defenders of order during a time of upheaval.

The Strike

Democracy is negated with the spread of strikes and wildcat uprisings. The outbreak of action is not conditional on a democratic poll of the rank and file or their representatives.

A fraction of the workers, because they are the most combative and least alienated elements situated in the most advantageous conditions, revolt. There is no gap between decision and execution, between those who decide and those who act.

The fundamental problem is not necessarily that of rallying the whole population behind the revolution. From a key position in the production process it is possible to make the capitalists yield. Work stoppages could be a self-reinforcing objective; all it takes is an unauthorized break or a refusal to do a particular job.

It is possible that a breakthrough staged by a handful of people could provoke a generalized breakthrough. This is what we witnessed on the scale of an entire nation in May 1968.

The strike movement spread. A majority of the workers supported it. Their support was generated in the heat of the struggle rather than having been secured in advance by means of a poll of those who were affected by the strikes.

If the workers had been required to democratically decide beforehand whether or not to commence hostilities, perhaps they would have balked. A small number of people set the example and showed them the way to cast aside their fear of the authorities and the possible consequences of their actions. They would be swept along by the atmosphere of struggle and solidarity and would be much more determined to overcome the feeling of discouragement and resignation engendered by the powerlessness of their everyday lives.

Let us imagine that the strike was decided on by means of a mass consultation. In that case it would most likely have taken a different course. The workers' offensive would have forfeited its unexpected quality. The enemy would have been informed of the nature, the form, the scale and the objectives of the movement. Organizational imperatives would have trumped action and would have muffled the independent initiative of the workers. The strikers would have remained more or less passive and, outside of the ranks of a minority of trade unionists or organizers, would have seen their strike as someone else's affair.

When workers begin to become radicalized, the democratic demand acquires more and more of the character of a demand for recuperation. A vote is held to decide whether or not to return to work. The bureaucrats, specialists in negotiation, seize the initiative.

Democracy becomes the expression of resignation. At this time it becomes visibly what it is in its essence.

Reliance on a general assembly as the only sovereign body is not enough to stem the tide of bureaucratization. The assemblies can become the privileged sites for manipulation, for mass meetings of atomized and powerless individuals, fortresses of confused and useless imposture.

General assemblies are necessary. It is necessary for them to be able to know where they stand, to assess their own forces, and to control and hold accountable their delegates and special committees. But the assembly must not take the form of something upon which all else depends, for whose benefit all the rest of reality loses all of its specific importance.

The Party

As the crisis of capital becomes more profound and the vanity of the capitalist solutions to the crisis becomes more obvious, a communist party will form within the population.

The formation of the party is not the cause that determines the outbreak of the crisis. It is only the prerequisite for the assault on capital. Its quantitative and qualitative development is, on the other hand, intimately linked to the emergence of this crisis. Its purpose is to facilitate the resolution of this crisis.

The party is not an association formed in accordance with a pre-established doctrine that will expand and grow without changing its nature. The party does not exist; it constitutes itself. It emerges slowly and proceeds by acquiring a clearer content and form. Its nature becomes more definite and its membership increases as the possibilities for breaking with the system become more apparent.

The constitution of the party is not, however, a new and unprecedented phenomenon. The party, as it is born at a particular historical moment, is the resurgence of a movement that transcends the limitations of this historical period. The modern party picks up the thread of a party whose reality and even memory have been erased by the counterrevolution.

During non-revolutionary periods, when communism can only be asserted timidly and haltingly, the party in the strict sense is condemned to remain an insignificant and forgotten fraction of the population. Alongside the conscious communists there are numerous unconscious communists who reveal themselves by their revolutionary actions. The party, in the fullest sense of those who demonstrate their more or less conscious commitment to communism in the increasingly frequent social conflicts, is invisible. Its image is not embodied within the reigning spectacle. Even at the level of this spectacle, however, its power is felt. Propagandists and politicians, in order to push their commodities, broadcast a distorted echo of its hopes. Bourgeoisie and bureaucrats tremble before this still nameless and faceless threat.

It is contradictory to claim to be a communist in a world that rejects communism by every means at its disposal. Communists are not supermen who already live in a different way than the rest of their fellow men. They do not remain untouched by the reigning misery. Their theoretical consciousness is of little avail in their attempts to transform their own lives.

It is essential, and perhaps inevitable, that conscious communists should appear and that they should endeavour to understand and to prepare for the communist revolution. But it does not make sense to oppose conscious communists to unconscious communists. What is important is to see how and why the conscious communist arises as a practical necessity.

There are certainly people who call

themselves revolutionaries. The production of these "revolutionaries" is not independent of the escalation of the crisis. Most of them are not communists and do not even know what they are and what they want. The desire for revolution appears as the last and the most vapid of all possible desires in this society. It is an abstraction separated from concrete needs and expectations. The "revolutionary" can discourse about everything and passionately engage in strategic disputes, but he is incapable of defining what it is that he wants. IF he speaks of immanent transformations, his perspective is dominated by the question of power. The society he wants to build rests upon a redistribution of power. What he "wants" is people's power, workers' power, students' power, the power of the councils (+ electrification or automation!), the power of the people over their own lives, the power of...

When the revolution corresponds to concrete needs and possibilities, however, the majority of those who will be revolutionaries will not feel the need to call themselves revolutionaries.

Only during a phase of open confrontation, when there is a possibility of communizing the social body, will the party be able to cease to be merely an association based on shared opinions or sporadic actions. It will finally be able to become a community of action.

When the great majority of the proletariat participates in the revolution, the party will not mistake itself for the class, since it does not claim to be the proletariat or to represent it. It is the most resolute and lucid fraction of the class. It coexists, collaborates with or confronts other fractions that are more moderate or that have an interest in the bourgeois apparatus or ideology.

Its action can be characterized in one sentence: to create a situation that makes turning-back impossible.

It is normal for there to be a lack of convergence between the action of the communists and the behaviour of the masses. This does not indicate a fundamental conflict. The party does not have to eliminate the mass organizations or movements. The councils and other base committees do not have to eliminate the party. If one of these things should happen it would necessarily signify the end and downfall of the revolution. This perception of such a conflict is a legacy of the Russian revolution and the councilist wave of the twenties. It has one defect: it perceives certain organizations as communist which were not communist.

The party will fight for the councils, since this struggle cannot be dissociated from the struggle for communism. This is true even if, with regard to this or that point or mode of organization the communists do not agree with the masses.

The party itself, which is not an organization, or worse, an institution managed from the top-down, will organize itself in the councilist manner. It is the community of those who stand for, beyond immediate tasks and interests, the defence of the movement as a whole. It must indicate the fortress to be stormed, it must concentrate its forces at strategic points, and it must propose solutions.

There is presently no organization that can call itself "the party". The latter can never be identified with a sect or any kind of mass organization. The supporters of communism are revealed by what they do rather than by membership in any particular group. Organizational forms do not have to be established or laid down in advance. They will be discovered during the course of the movement.

7. Insurrection and Communization

The communization of society will not be gradual or peaceful, but abrupt and insurrectionary. Nor will it take the form of a steady advance that will progressively unite the necessary forces.

Insurrection and communization are intimately linked. There will not be, first the insurrection, and then—made possible by the insurrection—the transformation of social reality. The insurrectionary process draws its power from communization itself.

There will not be a mixed or an intermediate mode of production between capitalism and communism. The period of transition and, before that, the period of rupture, are characterized by the contradiction between absolutely communist methods on the one side and, on the other, a reality that is still completely imbued with mercantile ways. It is in this phase that a society of abundance and freedom must confront the problems of poverty and power. It will have to liquidate the human and material consequences of an era of slavery and neutralize the forces that remain bound to that era.

Violence

The use of violence to attain their goals: this is what distinguishes revolutionaries from reformists.

The opposition between revolutionaries and reformists is not so much a matter of strategy and methods as it is a matter of the nature of the transformation that is to be brought about. This is what evidently causes a difference in their methods.

History distinguishes two types of reformists: the soft and the hard.

The soft reformists, social democrats and parliamentarists, think that their schemes can be realized in a gentle way. They were often right, as long as their illusions were proportional to the scale of the reforms that could possibly be obtained. Constantly, and from every corner of the world, they prove that the ruling interests will not engage in the repression of those who do not threaten them. These soft reformists sometimes turn hard, but then their hardness is for the most part directed against the proletariat.

Along with the soft reformists who turn hard, there are the real hard reformists, that is, the Stalinists and their ilk. These reformists consider themselves to be revolutionaries and their goal is to seize state power and control the economy by replacing its current managers. They have no interest in underestimating the striking power of their enemies. This is a matter of success and of saving their own skins at the same time.

And the revolutionaries?

A communist revolution is an enormous social upheaval. It entails confrontations and violence. However, while the revolution is an act of force, its essential problem is not the question of violence, nor is the precondition for its success essentially a question of military force.

This is because the revolution is not a question of power. We shall not fight over the state or the economy with the powerful on the playing field of power. Thanks to the positions that it occupies in the economy, communism will be able to undermine the foundations of and disarm the military counterrevolution. It will avoid, as far as possible, direct confrontation.

The communist revolution does not make violence the main problem, because it seeks to help that which already exists to burst forth, rather than to force reality to conform to a plan.

We are opposed to the fanatics and fetishists of violence as well as to the pacifists. Just as non-violent methods can and must be adopted, even with relation to enemy military forces, we must also reject the ideology of non-violence.

This ideology transmits and is based on pedagogical illusions. It assumes that everyone can be educated for non-violence and can be mobilized from scratch. It wants mass actions but does not see that the problems of information and coordination that this type of action poses, and the possibility of counterattack, cannot be resolved without possibly giving rise to violence. Systematic non-violence assumes that there is a consensus observed by enemies to respect certain rules and, above all, that there is a minimal freedom of information.

Non-violence is above all effective as a defensive method. Its limitations become apparent when it is a question of taking the initiative and of neutralizing the enemy.

The more consolidated the revolution is in terms of force and lucidity, the more capable it will be of rallying the vacillating elements to its side and neutralizing its opponents. By understanding the limited yet essential role of violence it can avoid mistakes that would entail bloody consequences.

The proletariat cannot renounce obtaining, manufacturing and using weapons. While weapons are not always scattered throughout a society, the materials from which they are manufactured are often available in large quantities. It is essential to find out where they are and to prepare ourselves for their eventual use, to arm ourselves and to prepare ambushes that will make our enemies pay a high price for their attacks. It would be ridiculous and shameful to incite people to form self-defence groups armed with revolvers and knives to defend their factories or their neighbourhoods against armoured vehicles and aircraft.

Future insurrections cannot be predicted or

stage-managed in advance but it is possible to advocate a strategy prior to or during the course of the movement. This strategy is based on knowledge of the nature of the communist revolution and of the forces at the disposal of each side.

The bourgeoisie and the bureaucrats have an army. The power of the proletariat resides in its economic position.

The army is vulnerable not so much from a military point of view as by virtue of its dependence on the economy. It is becoming increasingly more reliant on the economy with regard to its need for weapons, munitions, food and transport. It contains workers and technicians within its ranks. In order for it to wage war—and modern war is very expensive— it requires an uninterrupted supply chain, and the population of the country must continue to work.

The military counterrevolution must be attacked in its economic rear-guard. It is of crucial importance to prevent the national army from intervening in other countries for repressive purposes by compelling it to remain in its own country to maintain social peace.

The military commanders understand the risks involved if they attempt to compensate for the "shortcomings" of the workers in the domain of production. The army cannot organize the economy against the workers; it prefers to have a well-defined adversary of the same nature as itself, instead of performing tasks that are alien to it, and losing its way and being dispersed.

The Army

The revolution is commonly imagined as a clash between two armies: one following the orders of the privileged and the exploiters; the other at the service of the proletarians. According to this view, the revolution is reduced to a war. Strategy is reduced to the seizure of power and the control of territory. This is a dangerously false view that is based on the memory of the battles of the Russian and Spanish civil wars as well as the wars for national liberation.

Although it may happen that at one time or another, in this or that circumstance, revolutionary action may take a military form: commando attacks, aerial raids ... this will not change anything of the profound nature or the global character of the conflict.

To conceive of the revolution as a confrontation between red and white armies is not communist, but stupid, in view of the disproportionality of the military forces involved. To engage in such a war with capital would be to play the enemy's game.

The army and the police are the last defences

of capital. Their actions can be directly expressed in the form of the destruction of men and things but also by the creation and defence of a situation of misery that is conducive to the spread of egoism, fear and other primitive reflex reactions. This turns the impoverished populations against the revolutionaries (who are viewed as the cause of these problems) and tends to instil new life into the mechanisms of the mercantile society.

The army can be used to operate and control certain strategic sectors of the economy.

Due to its hierarchical nature, which rules out debate and dissent, which are replaced by obedience and discipline, and due to its patriotic purpose and ideology, the army tends to be a conservative institution.

The military counterrevolution does have its weaknesses, however.

The sense of self-confidence and the feeling that they have the law on their side, which are engendered among the military forces in their own particular ghetto and as a result of their *esprit de corps*, can neither be justified nor reinforced in a confrontation with an enemy army on a well-defined battlefield. The army must be prevented from functioning as an army; it must be opposed by the dissolving fluidity of communism. This entails paralyzing, contaminating, dividing, and disarticulating the military forces.

Our military attacks must be intimately linked with our activity of social destruction and reconstruction. The use of violence must not be transformed into an independent, self-justifying activity. Its purpose is to put a stop to or clear the way for situations directly in the interest of communization, which provides its justification as well as its power.

Before or during an insurrectionary phase, we can never be too mistrustful of separate violence and of terrorism. In terrorism, the revolutionaries are caught in the gears of attack and of counterattack, and communism is absent. When violence is transformed into violence for communism, rather than violence that accompanies communism, when it is vacated of its immediate content, all provocations are permitted. It is easy to commit murders and bombings and then blame the revolutionaries.

By way of the immediate and radical transformation of social organization we have to pull the rug out from under the feet of the military and deprive them of anything to defend. The army is an instrument of violence; it cannot do everything on its own because it is simply an organization for violence. We can do anything with a bayonet except sit on it.

It is a favourite preconception of the left to favour the intellectuals and to look down upon the military. Whenever a revolution takes place leftists think, quite naturally, that the former will be in favour of the revolution and the latter will be against it. On the one side intelligence, on the other brute force.

History shows just how erroneous such preconceptions are. Since the Paris Commune, when Colonel Rossel joined the insurrection and was shot for having done so, and when the progressive authors George Sand and Emile Zola violently condemned the insurrection, it has been common for one part of the armed forces to join the side of the revolution and for a no less significant part of the intellectuals to turn against it.

Such is the revolution: sometimes it horrifies those who support it, and fills those who dread it with enthusiasm.

The army forms its own separate institution whose values are, in part, alien to bourgeois or commercial values. Unlike the class of feudal lords, the bourgeois class is no longer capable of fighting in its own defence: it entrusts this task to the army and the police. Although one part of the army's leaders completely identifies its interests with those of the ruling class, there must be a latent contradiction between the interests and the customs of the military personnel and those of the bourgeoisie.

We must not allow ourselves to believe that the army, or any part of the army, will easily or spontaneously come over to the side of the revolution. This can only happen as the result of the development of the revolution itself and of its penetration of the army. The army will become revolutionary to the extent that, under the pressure of the soldiers and the policemen, the all-powerful hierarchy will be questioned and blind obedience condemned.

The revolutionaries must not make any concessions to militarism. The revolutionaries must make the soldiers understand that the latter are not fighting for their own interests, and much less for those of the Nation. They have to show them that their ideals are subverted by capital. They must also show them that the military personnel, as human beings, and their qualities and abilities, have a place in the communist movement.

Our goal is the destruction of the army. It is necessary that this be achieved with as little confrontation with the military as possible. The recently formed or reconstituted armed groups will gradually lose their military character through their participation in productive tasks and in the workers' councils.

The revolution must not ignore its dimension of force nor must it miss any chances of integrating into its forces, by transforming them, the institutions of repression of the old society. A policeman might be ready to serve a power that no longer seems to be subversive to him but instead looks like a new authority. Or it could be that some of them might not want to continue to be lackeys.

In any event, the revolutionaries and the proletarians must not allow others to possess a monopoly on force. This question of the arming of the proletariat will be a test that will allow us to judge the effectiveness of the connection of the military with the revolution.

Vengeance

The revolutionaries do not have a taste for blood, nor a spirit of vengeance. The revolts of the past show that blood was indeed spilled, but only a very small share of that bloodletting was due to the actions of the insurrectionaries. Hope extinguishes hate.

It was the counterrevolution that massacred, imprisoned and deported. Blood flowed during battles but often also, after the fighting was over, when military victory was assured. Murderous fury was born from the terror of the owning classes. The reaction had to crush the enemy forces. To them, the revolution seemed to reside in the revolutionaries. Therefore, the latter had to be destroyed.

The spirit of vengeance might play a role in workers' revolts. But that is all it was, compared to the repression carried out by the forces of Versailles, by the Kuomintang in 1927, by Franco's forces....

The workers' uprisings have been much less characterized by vengeance than were the anti-feudal peasant rebellions. This is because the revolution is not an act of desperation. Acts of destruction of goods and reprisals against persons are often the work of those who do not see any way out of their misery and who are satisfied with annihilating those who embody their oppression.

Vengeance is not just petty, but stupid. It condemns our enemies in advance on the basis of their past and reinforces their resolve to oppose us, out of fear and determination to survive. And it makes enemies among those who, rightly or wrongly, feel that they, too, have done something incriminating. And it encourages a situation in which personal grudges can be settled.

We must offer our enemies the opportunity to change sides. Communist principles do not in and of themselves dictate a uniform mode of conduct.

To the contrary, they imply that it is possible to express a diversity of characters, situations and past histories of those who participate in the revolution. More precisely, they imply that, just as our enemies do not view us as anything but "red vermin", we must for our part continuously strive to recognize even the worst of our enemies as human beings. Without any illusions about human nature.

It would be stupid to attack doctors, engineers, peasants, since many of these people would soon join us without our having to make any concessions to the myth of the specialist, to a hierarchy of labor, or to property. This means that the councils should sometimes protect the possessions of certain people. This will contradict the principle of equality but it will make it possible for some people to come over to the side of the councils by offering to allow them to keep something they value. The doctor could be guaranteed the use of his residence and of his professional equipment on the condition that he does not emigrate and that he treats those who need medical assistance. Certain second homes, located in the countryside, could be returned to their legal owners, or handed over to their parents or their friends, without thereby allowing anyone to possess two homes when others are living in broken down shacks.

On the other hand, those who seek to preserve their privileges or take advantage of the situation to feather their own nests must know that they will not be able to benefit from the mercy of their victims.

The more securely consolidated the revolutionary councils are, the more capable they are of decreeing clear rules and rapidly transforming reality, the less necessary the use of violence.

Reconversion

Communization does not mean expelling the bosses from the factories so that we can take their places, but rather begins with closing down many of the currently existing enterprises.

The line between the counterrevolution and the revolution will be drawn between those who, in the name of the fatherland, of democracy, of self-management, of the workers' councils, of Christ the King or chocolate pudding, incite the worker-consumers to cling to their activities as beasts of burden and to their drugs, and those others who incite them to massively reduce and to radically reconvert production. It is a matter of reducing pollution and of breaking as much as possible with the brutalization of labour and with the pseudo-abundance of commodities.

To remain in the factory, even for the purpose of self-managing it, is to freeze the situation to the benefit of the counterrevolution. And this would be the outcome whether this view is professed by fanatics of labour, by naïve trade unionists or by clever capitalists who are trying to gain time.

The revolutionaries will probably be accused by all these holy apostles of seeking to disorganize production and to reduce the standard of living of the people.

This scaling back of production must not be perceived as any kind of fascination with austerity. Such a policy would require far fewer sacrifices than any other solution; false solutions that would merely prevent a decisive break with the past and which would immobilize forces that are necessary for the struggle; false solutions that would allow all those who fear that the foundations of their power are disappearing to regroup: recalcitrant trade unionists, petty or big bosses, politicians, managers, employers....

Merely by ceasing the production of a myriad of useless, barely useful or harmful products, and tearing down the walls between enterprises, we could concentrate the forces required to produce indispensable or necessary products in abundance.

It will be necessary to undertake new research and begin a new kind of production. Communization does not mean, therefore, only the demonetization, but also the rapid transformation of production. These two things are intimately linked.

Blue-collar workers, office employees and teachers will be invited to take up jobs where they will be really useful. These changes will be based, first of all, on the spontaneous aversion of the masses for work and on the revealing of their own abilities. This will not take place under the aegis of a directive centre but will arise from many different initiatives. This does not mean that disorder will be given free rein. Every revolution implies some oscillations, and a certain amount of pandemonium and confusion. But such disturbances must be reduced to a minimum. And this is the task of the most radical elements. We are neither against order, nor against discipline, nor against organization, nor even against authority. Those who conflate revolution with confusion must be combated just as resolutely as the statists. Indeed, the former play into the hands of the latter.

Reconversion must above all allow for the satisfaction of the most basic needs. Then it must favour, above the production of certain products, the production of the tools and machines that are needed for their production. These materials will be distributed among the population and will permit each person to engage in manufacture on his own or else find others with whom he can manufacture things.

These are only some ideas concerning the possible modifications in the operation of major economic sectors. None of these transformations has any meaning in isolation. The peril of making concrete proposals resides in the fact that they could be turned against communism. But we cannot forget that revolutionaries cannot be content with articulating general principles but must, in accordance with the particular situation, offer concrete solutions.

Energy: there will be a significant reduction in the production of energy. This reduction will, most naturally, result from the shutting down of a part of industry that consumes the greater part of this energy. Perhaps these closures will be compulsory due to difficulties in assuring the supplies of oil, gas and coal.

The distribution of energy will be transformed. Part of the share of energy that was once utilized directly by industry can be transferred to domestic consumption: for heating, illumination and to provide power for small machines.

New sources of energy will gradually be

introduced. They must be developed in order to reduce pollution and to conserve limited resources such as fossil fuels. Perhaps a decentralized and intermittent form of production will be favoured for local use. This does not mean, however, that communism is fundamentally opposed to nuclear energy. It is simply a matter of establishing serious guarantees for the conditions of production and the needs for the use of energy. In the short term – water, wind or sun would be preferable.

Transport: means of transportation waste energy, constitute sources of pollution, crystallize social inequalities ... in this sector, too, there will have to be a significant degree of scaling back and rationalization that will enable a new use of space. People will have to organize themselves in order to avoid having to go on long journeys. There will be fewer occasions for people to travel against their will. The expansion of free time will make it possible for them not to have to spend so much of their time in their vehicles.

The production of automobiles can be halted. The number of vehicles presently in circulation, if they were to be used more rationally, would give us the time we need to develop and manufacture better machines. Some of these vehicles could be used as taxis, with or without assigned drivers, or they could be used for public purposes.

The great majority of vehicles will probably continue to be used privately. This will allow for the adaptation of traditional habits and give those who still have cars an incentive to keep them in good working order. The continued use of automobiles may be limited by certain conditions placed on their use in order to restrict or eliminate traffic in some locations and allow the most effective and advantageous possible use of those areas.

The trains and other modes of mass transport should be favoured and developed. These methods are safer, more energy efficient, and would involve less traffic congestion than individual means of travel. Our powerful and comfortable cars could be complemented with slower vehicles that would be more flexible and more suitable for individual use and would be equipped with non-polluting motors.

In the meantime, we can continue to produce trucks, bicycles, roller skates and good shoes.

To reduce the need for travel, mainly with regard to high-speed, long-distance contacts, we will have to develop a good telephonic or videophonic network. This will allow, at a very low cost, many more people to be in contact with each other than is possible today [this has since taken place—Note of the Portuguese Translator]. The airplane is a noisy mode of transportation, which produces a lot of pollution, for businessmen and tourists on tight schedules. Its use is not easily made generally available to everyone. We must therefore either eliminate it or limit its use to particular cases.

For long-distance travellers, because they cannot return to their fashionable vacation spots, should we bring back the great sailing ships? Their construction would lead to a healthy kind of competition. In any event, there are other ways to get from one continent to another: you do not need supersonic jet aircraft.

Publishing: this is a sector whose revolutionary importance is very easy to understand. Who will control the press?

In insurrectionary periods it is often the case that the workers' control the content of the newspapers that they print. This will once again take place, no matter how much it may displease the apostles of the freedom of the press who often are nothing but defenders of the freedom of money. This is not enough, however. The press must undergo transformations and must cease to be the contemplative reflection of reality.

The revolution will allow a freedom of expression that is impossible for us today. A large number of small printing machines, which belong to businesses and administrators, will be placed at the disposal of all.

Tomorrow, the whim of an editor will not determine whether a book or a text will be published. Its production, and then its printing, will be directly the affair of those who are interested in it. Its success will therefore depend on the determination of its author and the practical support for his project that he encounters.

Today, a considerable part of the cost of a book is accounted for by the expenses involved in its advertising and promotion. Here, the advantage of communism is obvious. We can even allow, in order to economize on wood pulp, that newspapers or other texts should be passed on from one person to another or else posted in public places.

Communism, in order to favour everyone's written, oral or audio-visual self-expression, must make provisions for reducing the social costs of paper and ink.

What will become of literature? It cannot be doubted that it will be transformed and that the production of romance and fantasy novels will gradually become unnecessary. We will therefore no longer have to continue to devote ourselves to fiction, to a world of books opposed to the real world. Perhaps some day, after the passage of a certain amount of time, written communication will lose its importance and will tend to disappear.

Construction: the construction industry will be transformed. This does not mean that the masons will be put out of work. Construction is one of the rare activities that does not regress.

Nonetheless, measures will have to be taken to limit, or more radically, to prohibit, construction in overpopulated cities and suburban areas. The people who move out of the urban centres, however, must be housed. Houses and buildings of every type will have to be built. It will also be necessary to demolish existing buildings and organize the recycling of their materials.

In this field, as in other activities, but perhaps even more rapidly, professional exclusiveness will be undermined. Anyone who wants to have a new house will have to roll up his sleeves and get to work. He will have the help of those who, due to their training or the experience, know how to do the work.

The homeless and ill-housed will immediately be moved into apartments and houses that for one reason or another are unoccupied. The suspension of rent payments and the cancellation of debts will naturally be one of the first acts of the revolution.

Clothing: We cannot transform everything all

at once. We will have to continue to produce what we can given the existing materials and machinery. There will, of course, be many changes with respect to the quality and durability of products.

A certain number of types of clothing and shoes can be produced in large quantities. In addition, the production of fabrics and small machines will be encouraged so that people can manufacture the clothing that they need, or that will allow the mass produced products to be adapted to the taste of the people and will also make possible the distribution of clothing in accordance with the effort expended on its production.

Food: the industrialization of food products has generally led to a decline in their quality. Communism must increase, as rapidly as possible, the quantity of food produced, change its mode of distribution in such a way as to benefit the undernourished populations of the third world, and undertake measures to improve the quality of the food that is produced.

Changes will be made with regard to the ingredients of the food products. Everything that is harmful or even useless and which only serves the purpose of deceiving the consumer must be excluded. Packaging will be simplified.

With regard to agriculture, the use of chemical

products must be limited and progressively reduced. This is not a matter of taking a principled position against everything chemical or artificial but of opposing the deterioration and falsification of agricultural products.

Monoculture must give way to poly-culture and to the combination of agriculture and animal husbandry, which will permit recycling and the use of manure and wastes. This will allow for the reduction of the volume of external inputs (chemical fertilizers, etc.), which is of vital importance especially for the underdeveloped countries.

It is preferable for the forces of society to be directly invested in working the land, instead of being devoted to factories producing chemical fertilizers and other chemical products. If labour is diverted from agriculture, it would be most effectively used to manufacture agricultural tools and machinery. This material must, for the most part, be introduced into the agricultural operations of the third world.

The research that is today devoted to improving the quality of food and the effectiveness of agricultural methods, research that is currently severely underdeveloped, must be intensified. The best varieties of plants, the best methods of tilling the soil, and the best mix of types of agriculture in accordance with the population's need for food, must be selected. There are plenty of things that need to be done in agriculture: should we favour the production of animal protein or plant protein? Should we emphasize productivity or small scale, traditional production methods?

Health: Health problems are largely caused by living and working conditions. Communism, by revolutionizing these conditions, will do a great deal of good for the health of the population.

Priority must be granted to hygiene and prevention. The production of drugs will be reduced. Certain products that are useless or that currently seem to be useful will be abolished. Just like brands of detergents, there are many different brands of the same pharmaceutical product. The cost of packaging and of advertising is added to the cost of the actual product. Obviously, all of this will disappear.

Medicine will be deprived of its professional exclusiveness as rapidly as possible, which means that a lost medical and health knowledge will be reintroduced among the population. This will make possible the utilization of medicinal plants, which would entail the training of a fraction of the population so that its members may engage in clinical practice within a very short time.

Education: The period of insurrection and reconversion will entail the need for education and training. At that time a large part of the population will be obliged to change its activity and everyone will have to multiply the tasks that they must learn.

This training will be carried out largely on the job. Each person will have to transmit his knowledge to his comrades.

Television and radio will make it possible to transmit, at low cost, the training that these people need. It is easy to broadcast courses in mechanics, agriculture and masonry in order to complement practical on the job training.

And what about the teachers? There will be no question of prohibiting them from teaching, but anyone who is not a teacher will not be discouraged from teaching, either, by any means. In any event, a large part of culture will not be the object of teaching in the strict sense of the word. With respect to children, there will be no question of withdrawing them from the care of those educators who are really devoted to their profession. However, from the moment when activities that are open to children begin to multiply and when these activities no longer require adults to be chained to professional or domestic labor the rest of their lives, it will be impossible to keep the children in school.

The members of the teaching profession, in order to assure their own well-being, will have every reason to devote themselves, like everyone else, to practical tasks. If they do not, they are the ones who will have to pay the price. There can be no doubt that most teachers, who are being increasingly transformed into teaching machines, will appreciate a new way of life that does places no obstacles in the way of their benefiting others with their knowledge.

Religion: Some of those "of little faith" claim that the communist revolution will make religion disappear. Even the Lord's ability to look after his own affairs is begrudged to him. As for us, we will let Him look after His own affairs.

Rupture

There will be no transitional stage between capitalism and communism, but rather a stage of rupture in which revolutionaries must seek to implement irreversible measures.

There are those who complain about the commodification and industrialization of all of social life. They want things to change but seek to be reasonable. They issue appeals for change to the authorities or to the official opposition. Above all, they want things to be changed in an orderly fashion. For them, the eruption of the masses on the stage of history merely implies an even more inextricable level of disorder.

They want to carry out a gradual de-commodification of the economy, developing public services and free distribution of goods. Wage labour will be reduced and, along with it, less dehumanizing productive activities will be furthered.

The more daring and bold among them plan, in the short term, the disappearance of the market and wages.

It is always the same hope to be able to use and control capital. The same illusion is propagated by those who want to preserve the wage system and at the same time eliminate wage differentials by transforming the wage into a fair remuneration based on the arduousness of each particular job.

Capital is fundamentally expansionist and imperialist. It therefore tends to seize all of social life. A non-mercantile sector that functions alongside the mercantile system will rapidly be re-mercantilized. It will continue to be a luxury and a game that is as completely dependent on capital as today's do-it-yourself trend, or else it will expand and, by virtue of its own productive contribution to circulation, it will then reinvent capitalism on its own. It will then undergo internal decomposition as well as external attack. The "free" producers, the weekend artisans who continue to be prisoners of a bourgeois way of life, will quite naturally seek an income from their parallel production in order to improve their bottom line at the end of the month.

Do we have to rely on political power to support such a "revolution"? This would be to forget the dependence of political power on the economy. It would amount to opposing mercantile totalitarianism with state totalitarianism.

Can we count on a spiritual transformation? This would be to believe that commodity society is, above all, a spiritual deviation. People's minds are what the situation allows them to be.

We cannot have one foot in the new world whilst keeping hold of our wallet.

These reformist conceptions do not understand anything about the need for a global rupture or about the nature of revolutionary proletarian action. They do not see that it is the situation and the activity of the class of the dispossessed that is the real enemy of the commodity system. They think that one can take measures against capital because they view it as a thing whose power has to be restricted, rather than a social relation.

Capital can amuse itself by opening up avenues of freedom to human activity and making it seem that it has been de-commodified. It sells us a new life at its vacation resorts, and you pay later for not having to pay now. The new systems of payment tend to avoid any direct and oppressive contact with money. All of these developments show the need and the possibility of communism, but also the recuperative, vampire-like and deceitful nature of capital.

The commodity system is a totality. It will be overthrown as a totality. It cannot be communized one sector at a time; all its sectors are intimately connected. In any case, can we really believe that anyone could limit the areas of intervention of an insurrection?

It is precisely the "anti-mercantile" measures that aim to temporarily restrict or to render the activities of capital less visible, that merely have the goal of dissuading or hindering an insurrection. Whether this is a result of the good intentions or even the lack of understanding of those who advocate such policies, they can only serve the counterrevolution.

In an insurrectionary period the revolutionaries must devote themselves to denouncing pseudo-radical measures and precipitating the course of events. Their actions will frequently be denounced, not for their revolutionary nature, but rather as excesses engaged in by those who disguise themselves as revolutionaries in order to all the more effectively combat the revolution.

The solution for the important problems posed by the sudden break with the commodity economy will be based above all on the councilist organization of production and distribution of goods. Who gets scarce products will no longer be determined by who has money, but, even in the intermediate stage, by the councils and committees of "consumers" who will seek to allocate goods in accordance with their best possible use. The danger lies in believing that we can establish a mixed system in order to avoid difficulties.

The councils will have to solve difficult problems but they will constitute the only force capable of solving them.

To make possible and to support councilist organization it will be necessary for the active wing of the revolution to concentrate its forces at certain strategic points. It will either destroy or permit the survival or the recovery of the old system.

The banking and financial system must be destroyed at their material foundations. We have to attack these institutions and burn their account books, their records and their archives. Everything that even looks like a means of payment will have to be destroyed.

The state machinery will have to be paralyzed. This is not to say that there will have to be a frontal assault on the heart of the system, but rather that its multiple tentacles must be destroyed. The state has its fingers in every nook and cranny and this is both its strength as well as its weakness

We have to attack everything that allows for the control of people and, first of all, identification documents of every kind. We will have to hunt down state and private archives. Apart from some documents of revolutionary or historical interest, all administrative archives and papers of every kind will have to be destroyed.

The seizure of the prisons and the freeing of the prisoners, including the political prisoners, will be the order of the day. This is sure to strike fear into the hearts of all but the most courageous; all the scum of the night will run through the streets. Are the prisons not crowded with terrible thieves and horrible murderers?

In fact, most prisoners are proletarians who sought, by attacking commodities and property, to escape from their condition. They are not, for the most part, either minor saints or big-hearted revolutionaries. Because of the nature of their crimes, however, they will disappear with the disappearance of the current system. They will know, in their overwhelming majority, how to place their talents at the service of the revolution.

And the underworld? Generally the real pariahs are not behind bars. Sometimes they even work with the complicity of the police. And what about the murderers? They often have the law on their side and are frequently found at the head of governments.

The liberation of the prisoners will not apply to the real scumbags and notorious counterrevolutionaries. With the end of commodity society, the organization of armed militias will allow for the reduction of the number of malefactors.

These different measures cannot be applied in just any context, nor in just any relation of forces. They will, however, be an imperious necessity for the revolutionaries and the anti-statists.

The committees responsible for the distribution of goods will be able to concentrate the small merchants and managers and use their shops. If these social categories demonstrate their willingness to participate in the reconversion, so much the better. If they resist and seek to continue to be owners of their stock and of their stores we have to do without them. In the case of privately stockpiled merchandise that is important and necessary, we will have to seize it from its owners. In any event, their power is limited because all we have to do is cut off their supplies.

We will be able to reconvert advertising into anti-advertising. This will consist of the dissemination of information about the characteristics and the manufacture of products, the state of reserves, and encouraging moderation.

Internationalism

The revolution will be global.

It is not a moral imperative: all men are equal and brothers and they have a right to this.

The revolution will be worldwide because capital itself is a worldwide reality. It destroys human communities, separates individuals, transforms every person into a competitor with everyone else. But it unites and unifies the human species through its action, through its own movement. Today, for the first time in history since Adam and Eve, there is a convergence between the genetic unity and the social unity of the species.

The birth of the national idea and of nation states is the direct result of capitalist development, of the destruction of traditional groups, of the standardization of exchange, of constantly growing inequality. But if capital protects itself behind its borders it cannot allow itself to be imprisoned within them. Its anonymous and imperialist development always has a tendency to conquer and unify markets. Different countries and regions successively assumed the privileged position in the accumulation of capital before entering into decline and giving way to others.

The contemporary epoch is witnessing the acceleration of this process. There is an ongoing process of globalization of commodity relations and an exacerbation of inequality. Colonization, world wars, the development of new poles of accumulation, the constitution of new nation states that are more or less pawns, are the stages of this process. The multiplication of nations and states will not impede their unification, not even at the political level. The small states will be subjugated by the stronger states. They will be regrouped in military alliances and economic zones. Global institutions and military strike forces will be formed.

Even more extraordinary is the internationalization of exchange and the formation of multinational corporations, which are overtaking political unification and depriving the states of a large part of their economic power. These gigantic enterprises are wealthier than many nations. They have a planetary view of things and seek to produce and to sell wherever it is most profitable without any concern for borders.

Trade is standardizing life all over the world and we find the same kind of cereals, the same kind of buildings, and the same kind of education all over the world. Local colour, protected or subsidized, is an aspect of advertising for the consumption of tourists and traditionalists. Nothing is more indicative of this idolatry of the national idea than the typical clothing styles spread throughout the world by similar aircraft. Here are some Frenchmen, over there, some Japanese Geishas ... and sprinkled a little all over, there are airborne Palestinian hijackers.

Faced with all of this, revolutionaries obviously cannot appeal to the defence or restoration of the fatherland, as is being done by a whole array of idiots and demagogues. Nor can we defend regionalist or neo-nationalist movements that advocate the formation of new, more legitimate fatherlands. Invoking the right to be different and autonomous, they oppose nationalism with nationalism, one state with another state. These movements are at first quite often healthy reactions against statism, standardization and the unequal development of the contemporary world. The only possible solution is to put an end to capital and to all of its states.

Communism is not the enemy of nations, if by love of country we understand man's bond with his region, his countryside, his customs, and his local way of life. We do not want to resuscitate the spirit of parochialism but we are against the levelling of countries and their inhabitants.

The defenders of the fatherland are often not at the same time defenders of the state. Their nostalgia wants to ignore that the latter seeks to destroy the values that they defend.

Paradoxically, nationalism thrives to the extent that the knowledge and the connection of man with his environment deteriorates. Nationalism values not a real community but the image of a community embodied in the fetishism of the flag or of the national hero. Our epoch is rendering all this bric-a-brac more and more unfashionable. The feelings that it embodies are increasingly more hypocritical or disconnected from reality.

Most of the leaders who exalt the national idea really do not give a damn about it. The ruling classes and the privileged have often demonstrated the scant importance that they grant to patriotism. The national interest is only valid when it corresponds with the interest of capital. As soon as a serious proletarian threat arises, the ruling classes of the different countries make haste to settle their differences.

The revolution will be worldwide because the problems that have to be resolved will be global problems. The interpenetration of the different economies prevents any of them from going it alone. In any event, if the revolution breaks out in one country it will have to confront the attacks of foreign counterrevolution. This interdependence, however, the highly developed means of communication, and the simultaneity of economic and political upheavals, will make the revolution more contagious than ever. Every state that sends police to our country must fear an uprising at home. The more rapidly the insurrection is generalized, the harder it will be to repress.

Hunger and pollution do not have local causes, it is just that their effects are localized. The revolution will have to establish universal rules for the protection of nature. Agriculture will have to be organized to respond to the needs of all the people of the world.

This does not mean that the rich, industrialized countries suck all the blood from the poor countries or that the poor countries will be dependent on the privileged zones.

Each region must, depending on its problems and its resources, and the importance of its proletariat, find organizational forms and its own paths of development. Each region should also solve as many of its problems as possible on the basis of its own resources.

In the meantime it will be necessary, especially at first, to organize transfers of materials and technicians to help the most disadvantaged regions to overcome their tragic poverty as quickly as possible. If necessary, the consumption of food in certain regions will have to be reduced or modified in order to assist other regions. The communists will always be in the vanguard of the struggle against local egoism.

The underdeveloped countries can be communized, despite their low levels of development. The possibility of communism is established on a world scale. What matters is not so much the quantitative development of the productive forces as their qualitative development. A certain technical and scientific level will engender quantitative abundance in the short term. The current dominance of the developed countries will help usher in the dawn of communism, in supporting local proletarian forces to liquidate capital everywhere.

How can communist transformations be promoted in countries that are predominantly agrarian? We cannot resort to primitive accumulation. Unlike capitalism, communism will not be established by overthrowing traditional social structures. It will, to the contrary, be capable of establishing its foundations on the basis of certain structures by liberating them from their most negative aspects, rediscovering under the parasitism and feudalism of these structures the underlying peasant communities.

This will not prevent the parallel development of modern activities. At the heart of these communities, technology can be introduced: small-scale agricultural machinery, energy systems, birth control, preventive medical care.... There will not be any absolute incompatibility between traditional communitarian equilibrium and the use of simple technologies. Even now, there are cases where primitive populations understand how to use modern technologies. The real disadvantage is, rather, the disintegration of these communities by the action of capital.

It is virtually certain that the populations in question and their social structures will continue to develop. But this development will not mean the destruction of men and the negation of communitarian values.

Can we expect to base our hopes on the foundation of worldwide solidarity with its base in the working class? Is it not the case that the workers are often racists?

Often workers act like racists. Racists against foreigners and above all racists against migrant workers or racial minorities. We see "working class" governments prove that they are more racist, especially when it comes to immigration, than bourgeois governments. It is often the business class that is in favour of immigration or of abolishing racially discriminatory laws.

Working class racism corresponds, first of all, to an attitude of an oppressed person who, not being capable of escaping his condition, is content to feel superior to his dog, to a cop, or to an immigrant. It is the expression of a real class interest, of the working class as a commodity. The intellectual can talk as much as he wants about human brotherhood. The worker, especially the unskilled worker, knows well enough that the foreigner is first of all his competitor in the labour market. Open or latent racism is born from the inability to recognize that it is capital that sets the wage workers against each other. This lack of understanding is not merely the expression of a simple intellectual deficiency. It corresponds to impotence. Understanding and the ability to change reality go hand in hand. To the extent that the proletariat advances and becomes unified racism falls by the wayside. It is not necessary to wait for the revolution: in partial struggles, the workers of different origins reject prejudices and mutual mistrust.

8. Proletariat and Communism

Communism is the negation of the proletarian condition by the proletarians themselves. The proletariat and communism are realities that are intimately and contradictorily linked. If we separate them we can understand neither the communist movement nor the proletarian revolution.

Lenin

Lenin, following Kautsky, said that the proletarians are not capable, on their own, of going beyond a trade unionist consciousness. They can merely dream of selling themselves for the highest price, but not of the revolutionizing of society. Lenin was wrong. Proletarians are incapable of attaining a clear awareness of their economic interests. Proletarians are commodities but they are also unsuccessful merchants. In their struggle and in their business deals the proletarians endlessly demonstrate that they do not know what they want and that they mix up and confuse economic and human realities.

This is a drawback, because with respect to the defence of their economic interests, the proletariat is much less effective than the bourgeoisie. But we cannot judge the proletariat according to a bourgeois standard.

Lenin was right to emphasize the discontinuity between trade union consciousness and revolutionary consciousness. The latter is not merely the most extreme version of the former. Both go hand in hand. Revolutionary consciousness, however, and for us this means communist consciousness, does not have to be imported from the outside, it is not a product of the intellectuals as a social category. Lenin's point of view is not stupid, as certain defenders of the people think, but merely takes account of what appeared to indeed be taking place. This appearance would be immediately contradicted by a period of revolution.

The proletariat shows every day that it is already beyond the economy. Its ineffectiveness and its naïve illusions are the negative and fleeting obverse of its humanity. In the struggle, and independently of the necessarily limited nature of its demands, the proletariat demonstrates in many ways, and with many lapses, its humanity and its aspiration towards communism.

What is of interest here is not what the proletariat is or seems to be when it is working, when it marches on May Day, or when it responds to opinion polls. Its fundamental situation will be require it, and already requires it, to act in a communist way.

In normal times the proletariat, in order to survive, must seek to compensate, in the thousands of ways that are available to it, for this fundamental privation. It finds interests, fatherlands, and drugs in the spectacle. It seeks to live vicariously through the power of its enterprise or of its trade union. Capital cannot abolish generalized prostitution, but it can entertain those who prostitute themselves. It consoles them by allowing them to "realize" themselves and deceive themselves in commodities and images.

The proletariat is not the positive embodiment of communism within capitalism. Nor is it permanently integrated for all of eternity within the system that sucks its blood and immiserates its life. Its reality is fundamentally contradictory. It seems to be integrated, while at the same time it blindly lurches towards communism. Suddenly it opens up a breach.

It rushes in and enlarges it. The consequences of its actions push it forward. It discovers its power and does things that it never would have dreamed that it was capable of doing.

Bourgeois and Proletarians

What is the proletariat? Where did it come from and where is it heading? What is its size?

With regard to the numerical significance of the working class, in the narrowest sense of the term, some assessments can be made on the basis of official statistics. It represents a small part of the world population; we can estimate it to consist of between 200 and 250 million individuals. This number, of course, does not account for the total number of proletarians insofar as it excludes the families of the workers, and due to the fact that it does not include a large number of proletarianized salaried workers, even in industry. In any event, the numerical significance of the working class, which is already enormous if we compare it to that of the bourgeoisie, does not tell the whole story regarding its real importance.

We must also point out that this importance, contrary to the theories that certain vanguard sociologists are advocating, is growing.

Like the bourgeoisie, however, the proletariat is not a thing that we can touch, define and count with precision. This does not diminish its reality at all, even if the sociologists cannot catch it in their academic nets.

We cannot reduce the proletariat to a standardized image: miserable starvelings, workers who are little more than monkeys, waving a red flag. It is only in certain situations that the workers' outlines clearly emerge.

Just as the bourgeoisie is defined as a caste, by its privileges and its special characteristics, by how hard it is to join its ranks, instead of as a class, so, too, is the proletariat reduced to a socio-professional category or an aggregate of socio-professional categories.

On the basis of such a definition it is easy to show that it is difficult, if not impossible, to define the proletariat. Does it really exist at all? Is it not the case that technological progress and social welfare measures have caused it to disappear? The class struggle, even if it is granted any importance, is reduced to just another kind of conflict. Male and female, young and old, town and country, are all engaged in conflict with each other. So why shouldn't the same be true of workers and employers?

Our sociologists accuse Marx of having invented the class struggle and of not understanding the concept of social class. He contradicted himself because sometimes he spoke of the peasants as a class and at other times he spoke of them as divided into opposed classes.

The fact that the peasants can be considered to be a single class because they have common interests and illusions, because they want the same things, and that these same peasants can be divided into poor and rich peasants, into farmers and landowners, transcends the understanding of a sociologist. The sociologist is not capable of understanding that a class cannot be defined, from either the intellectual or the practical point of view, independently of the activity that constitutes it as a class. There are no classes independent of the class struggle.

To reduce a class to a socio-professional category is to give the illusion of science and rigor. In fact, everything depends on two more or less arbitrary criteria that are chosen to divide the social body. Above all to reify reality.

Everything is reduced to the place that capital attributes to humans. A particular division is frozen in time: intellectuals, workers, residents of the poor suburban concentrations, those who earn minimum wage. In this way, neither the cause of these situations nor how they can be overcome is perceived.

Nor are those hypotheses any better which, accepting the fact that "classes" will always be classes, imagine that some classes will defeat others. In this view, in the west the bourgeoisie rules while in the countries of the east the proletariat establishes its dictatorship.

For us, the proletariat cannot be defined separately from its struggle against capital, that is, separately from communism.

This does not mean that a class is constituted by all the people who fight for the same cause. In that case, the bourgeois who sympathizes with the revolution is transformed into a proletarian and a reactionary street sweeper would be a banker. Anti-capitalism, that is, communism, can become a cause for many people but by its very nature it is not a cause. It is an activity linked to a particular social situation.

The proletariat is that fraction of the population that produces capital, and is separated from its ownership and control. The nightmare of self-management is making the proletarians perform bourgeois functions. This chimera is being implemented without having to abolish classes.

The bourgeoisie and the proletariat contradictorily coexist as a single group. The same man who tends to his machine will be his own enemy on the management council.

It is sometimes the case that, from time to time, children of the bourgeoisie ruin their health in the factories and workers increase the number of their possessions at the cost of some sacrifices. This has nothing to do with the abolition of classes.

There is a solid line of demarcation between the managers and the slaves of capital. It just so happens that some people have one foot inside that border and one foot outside of it. They have to choose one or the other.

Will it be necessary to define the dividing line? One could attempt to clarify it with reference to one's attitude towards money. It is of course true that bourgeois and proletarians can be distinguished by the quantity of money that passes through their hands. This is not good enough, however. Basically, the proletarian does not see money as just money. For him it represents a certain number of goods. For the bourgeois, money is money-capital. He uses money to make more money. He invests it and, lo and behold, it multiplies! It is this aspect that, spanning the centuries, unites the bourgeois of the middle ages with the modern manager. Today, however, we have to add hypocrisy.

To define the bourgeois class we also have to take into account its family relations and the sociological factors that transform its children and wives into bourgeoisie.

In economic life and in the environment of the enterprises, the border is between those who have access to financial knowledge and decisions—not necessarily the technicians and accounting staff—and the others. There are those who know that an enterprise is money that is momentarily immobilized, whose purpose is to produce more money. And there are those who, comprising the great mass, see a factory above all as an affair of use values.

Pigeonholing an individual in any given class is sometimes difficult. Any given manager, any engineer, or, why not, any worker, can, due to his family background, his chances for promotion, his position in the hierarchy, his wealth or his property, be co-opted by the ruling class. On the other hand, small businessmen are connected by a thousand connections to the ruled class.

From the revolutionary point of view it is important not to reject, from the start, and consign to the bourgeois camp, the wealthy proletarians. The engineer connected with the bourgeoisie and, for even more powerful reasons, to his colleagues who do not make as much money as he does, or who do not exercise his leadership role, or who do not have his connections, can feel the contradiction between his professional and human interests and the limits imposed by financial considerations. This could cause such people to sympathize with communism, and with a world in which technical planning is not subject to the dictatorship of exchange value.

Their knowledge and abilities are necessary. We must nonetheless be careful of those who might mistakenly choose to join the revolutionary side because they are aware of the fact that their condition is being proletarianized and they ingenuously expect to become new authorities.

In a normal period, and primarily outside of the process of production, the situation might not appear to be so well defined. Society seems to be composed of particular individuals who wander about in one direction or another. The worker and the bourgeois seem to disappear in order to be nothing but equal voters or consumers who have more or less money. When a conflict breaks out, when revolution makes its appearance, the particles group together around antagonistic poles.

The proletariat is not an undifferentiated mass. Certain social layers and individuals play a crucial role by virtue of their place in production and due to their own particular qualities. They more or less help the class to constitute itself as a class.

Some social layers are more restless than others or assert their discontent more openly. Appearances, however, can be deceiving. A group that is more turbulent than another could prove to be hardly revolutionary. There are those who protest for their own very personal reasons. They want to rebel because their status has declined inside the system. But they do not take aim at the foundations of society. They might even be more afraid of the prospect of a revolution than capital is.

Those who seem to be the most integrated, the most tranquil because they are spoiled by the system can, upon awakening, go right to the heart of the matter. The power and the self-confidence that their situation allows them could permit them to go on the offensive without any concessions to capital.

The development of individuals in social classes cannot be considered independently of the depth of the conflict and the situation as a whole. Some social layers, such as students, intellectuals, or executives cannot rise by their own efforts beyond a corporative consciousness or, even worse, a pseudo-revolutionary consciousness. If communism develops, these layers, by virtue of the lack of autonomy that characterizes them, will be radicalized. If they do not have the power to defend their real interests, they can only obtain that power by joining with and supporting the workers.

Will the immense mass of peasants of the third world be able to participate in the communist revolution? Is it part of the proletariat? Yes, but not due to the degree of its poverty. The more direct the influence of capital is over its existence, the more this mass of peasants is a part of the proletariat.

Even if the peasant is not a wage worker, he tends to join the class of the workers due to the increasing influence of the commodity economy on the totality of men and resources. The offensive of the wage earning proletarians will help him identify his enemy and the solutions to his problems.

Wage labour is, in a way, the ideal relation for the exploitation of capital. It is therefore not possible to identify proletarians as wage earners in general. We have already shown how the relations of slavery were integrated into the capitalist universe and were therefore transformed with regard to their content. Countless small proprietors are directly subjected to capitalist exploitation and are often more oppressed than wage workers. The directors of large enterprises are paid wages. Therefore, they are not bourgeoisie. They lay claim to a wage and this wage is only a small part of their real contribution.

Certain professions develop more revolutionary attitudes than others. It all depends, for the most part, on the degree of identification that exists between the worker and his function.

Some play the game. They do not distance themselves from the work they perform. That is when their work, as in the case of teachers, transforms them into its own instruments. That is why their professional role becomes, by their own efforts, their own role. This is the case when the product of their labour is not a product and contributes directly to the functioning of their enterprise.

In these two cases, there is a tendency for a justificatory ideology to develop from their professional function and its contradictions. The most alienated workers end up believing that, thanks to their own abilities or to the general usefulness of their work, they are revolutionizing society.

The most lucid workers are often those who do not feel connected to their enterprise or to the function that they exercise there. And this is true of most of the workers.

By virtue of their place in production, and the solidarity that is generated by their place in production, and from their human qualities, the workers are at the heart of the communist revolution. The American or Soviet worker, while it is easier for him to survive than it is for an Indian beggar, even if he is more corrupted, also occupies a better vantage point from which to recognize the nature of the oppression that weighs upon him and how to put an end to it.

It is customary to deny the working class its central role in the revolution.

Emphasis is placed on his absence from the struggles for national liberation that are in the meantime being waged by the Marxist states.

The absence of revolutionary consciousness among the masses of workers of the rich countries and the advantages they derive from the system are highlighted.

Other social categories are entrusted with the role that the workers seem to be unable to fulfil. The revolutions of the 19th century were the work of artisans. In the 20th century, the Leninist intellectuals had to take their place. In the countries of the third world it is the peasants who now play that role.

If one carefully examines these matters one will see that the workers were regularly at the heart of attempts to radically transform reality. They are accused of not having been involved in revolutions that were, in the final analysis, bourgeois. When they did intervene their activities played a secondary role behind the actions of the socialist groups that, from the beginning to the end, showed that they were hardly communist at all. This or that characteristic of the proletarians who participated in the revolutions is highlighted and exaggerated to show that they were workers of dubious backgrounds or marginals, farmers, petty bourgeoisie, soldiers, or rioters passing themselves off as workers.

The modernists replace a bourgeoisified proletariat with new categories. The revolution will be the work of the young people because they are not yet domesticated, the women because they are closer to life, the hippies and other marginals because they are outside the system, the blacks because they enjoy music and have rhythm in their blood ... while others do not see the need to privilege any particular category. Capital is a non-human power at the hands of which everyone is a victim and it is therefore humanity as a species that must revolt. There is no longer (or almost no longer) either a bourgeoisie or a proletariat.

This highlighting of the role of this or that social group or category of age or sex, is carried out on the basis of the values of which these groups are allegedly the bearers. There will not be so much an alteration of the choice of revolutionary subject as an implicit recognition of reality as it is. Young people will be revolutionary as young people, women as women, and as for the proletariat, which includes young people and women, it is revolutionary to the extent that it ceases to be a proletariat. The proletariat is not a social group. It is a movement. It is that which is transforming itself. It exists by virtue of its possibilities for self-destruction.

It is not that young people, women, sick people … do not have specific interests or that they are incapable of transforming reality. It is just that, except as proletarians, they can hardly defend their interests as young people, women, sick people, within any given reality. The proletarian revolution provides them with the means, without denying their ideas, to go beyond their specific demands and to surpass them. It is the young people, the women, and sick people, who act, but no longer for youth or femininity, or, on the other hand, for state subsidies and the respect of the citizens.

And the intellectuals?

In a way, the revolution demands that the proletarians become intellectuals. They must become capable of going beyond their immediate situation. Everyone knows that, at the high point of revolutions, debates are carried on in the streets concerning questions that were previously the preserve of the philosophers.

The revolution also means the end of the intellectuals as a separate social category. If the intellectuals participate in the revolution they can do so only by negating their own condition, by recognizing their partial, mutilated character. Eventually, measures must be taken to prevent them from even continuing to be intellectuals.

Intellectuals have often been attributed with a privileged role as the bearers of consciousness. By itself, consciousness is nothing and can do nothing. The intellectuals, who often think that they can rise so high as to achieve a general and objective understanding of things, often line up behind the established powers. They are subject to the worst illusions and they defend—with a critical spirit, of course—the worst outrages. They are ready to justify everything in the name of Reason, of History, of Progress.

The demands of the intellectuals serve more to encourage the bourgeoisie than the workers. It is much more noble to demand freedom of expression than to demand bread. The intellectual appears to be a defender of the general interest. The worker seems to be an egoist who is only concerned with worldly matters.

Proletarian demands, however, are more profound than those of the intellectuals. The latter specialize in demanding empty forms. When the workers demand or even impose freedom of expression, it is because they have something to say. Otherwise, the question is of relatively little interest to them. Their ability to refrain from dissociating form and content, to not fight merely for hot air, is a sign of communism. The problem with the intellectuals is that they often make their money from wind.

Young people are often the most active in revolutions. That this is perhaps due to biological causes rather than to their social situation is sufficient as an explanation. Even the ones who come from the privileged classes are less connected to the interests at stake. They have to wait for their inheritance! Capitalist society fetishizes youth and renewal but separates young people from positions of responsibility and property. They are therefore the most eager for revolution.

Besides the young, the marginal elements of the population are sometimes emphasized. They do not live like other people; are they not the future? In this case, too, there is an inability to understand that the revolution can and must arise from the heart of the system itself. This view reflects an inability to think dialectically regarding the proletariat and illusion concerning the level of independence of the marginals with respect to the system.

Will capital itself abolish the social classes, thus bypassing revolution? It has long been claimed that the bourgeois revolution would finally allow for all human beings to be equal.

The division of society into classes is healthy. Perhaps society has never enjoyed such good health, just as it has never used so many means to cause this fact to be forgotten.

Capital is, of course, an impersonal force. Everyone, to one degree or another, feels its effects. Even the poor bourgeois who works himself to exhaustion, who fights with his children, who breathes polluted air!

Some people have, more than others, the possibility of remedying the effects of capital. Unlike the general living conditions, these possibilities are today quite manifold. The opportunities for product diversification, the development of trade, are making it possible for certain groups of the population to have a level of consumption and a quality of life that are very different from and higher than that of their contemporaries. Maybe the bourgeoisie are not the happiest people but at least they can choose to cease to be bourgeois. An analogous decision is not possible for the street sweeper. If the bourgeoisie are not content with their own lifestyle, this is all the more reason to abolish this class and its society.

The bourgeoisie is not exhibitionist. It leaves exhibitionism to the *nouveaux riche*. Nor does it have any interest in showing off the life it leads in its *dachas* (Russian vacation homes in the country) and its private beaches. The proletarians have the habit of overestimating the wealth of the social classes with whom they associate in their everyday lives and underestimating the wealth of the real bourgeoisie.

Even if the bourgeoisie were to live a frugal and austere lifestyle, this would not make it disappear as a class. What counts is, above all else, its economic and social function. Their wealth is obviously connected with this function. A part of their consumption, even in western countries, is conflated with the expenses of doing business. They travel, they eat and they have sex on behalf of and at the expense of their companies.

Capital has a tendency, today more than ever, to corrode the identity of social groups. This is as true of the bourgeoisie as it is of the working class. The voter or the consumer is beyond class. The pleasure that he takes in his purchases is not linked to a status but to impersonal money. This capitalist negation of classes is helping to pave the way for a classless society. But this trend is itself negated by economic need, which tends to make wealth hierarchical and to separate functions.

The struggle of communism is not waged on behalf of any particular class but rather on behalf of humanity. This struggle is, however, directed against those who seek to negate all of humanity. The revolution will not be universally accepted and it would be dangerous to try to make people believe that it will. Maybe some bourgeoisie will join the movement but this will not alter in the least the fact that the interests of the bourgeoisie and of communism are mutually opposed. The proletarian revolution will gain immediately as the bourgeoisie are dispossessed. Communism is about the human species; but while there will be people who can identify their immediate interests with the species during a period of rupture, there will be others who cannot.

Waiting for Godot

What do revolutionaries propose to do whilst we are waiting for the big night?

We have no silver bullet for hastening the moment nor do we have an ideal line of conduct to defend. The communists are stuck, like everyone else, to the capitalist glue and are therefore incapable of designing a pure and universal strategy that would make the best use of individual interests, abilities and conditions. In any event, we do not propose that the "masses" should do anything we would not do, and vice-versa. We can merely point out differences in behaviour.

We are not at all purists and we accept reforms, however limited, if they are real. It is easy to show how strict one is when one is talking about the great victory, when it is paid for with a lot of hot air.

We are not at all purists and we accept action from the base with those who do not share our views, as long as the perspective of the action are clear.

It is advisable to be flexible on the practical level in order to be able to take advantage of constantly changing and unpredictable situations. We have to know how to compromise and, above all, how to recognize compromises for what they are. We do not have recipes to offer and we criticize those who need them. No robotic commandos!

Those whose action is accompanied by an obsession about being recuperated will be recuperated immediately, and radically. Sectarianism is, above all, a way for someone to protect himself against his own uncertainties. On the other hand, when one has profound convictions, not ideologies, one can innovate, improvise, and take action without feeling that one's purity is threatened. And if we make mistakes? It is not by wrapping oneself up, immobilized, in the truth, that the truth is preserved.

This pragmatic flexibility must be accompanied by a great deal of strictness and—we say this to shock the "free spirits"—even doctrinal dogmatism. Theoretical clarification and soundness are essential. We have to know where we are going and let other people know as well.

Our era is characterized by rigid behaviour patterns and flabby thinking. We need to break with this trend. Ideas only have interest if they provide sufficiently solid points of reference.

A classic question: should we participate in trade union activity? It all depends on the circumstances and on the people involved. But the trade unions are integrated into the system!? Maybe that would be a reason for someone to participate in them. He might want to take advantage of the benefits that trade union organizations provide, or he might want to demonstrate the limits of these benefits. Sometimes one can take a position right in the middle of the street and clearly show the contradiction between the revolutionary content and the trade union form.

While participation in the trade unions is acceptable, the conquest of the trade union apparatus for the purpose of transforming it in a revolutionary sense must be rejected.

In the struggle, provided that possibilities arise for us to organize in a broader and less specialized way, the trade unions must be rejected. The trade union form can be used in a situation of retreat but must not impede the further development or the intensification of the struggle. Action on behalf of the class must not be opposed to action on behalf of an organization of specialists in the formulation of demands or the conduct of negotiations. In any event, it is certain that as long as the workers are commodities whose price is subject to negotiation, the trade union structures will have a reason to exist.

Limited struggles that prepare the way for the final struggle must not be renounced. Nor should wage struggles be scorned, which constitute steps towards the abolition of wage labour. The economic bottom line manifests the capacity for resistance and can become dangerous for the system by threatening its heart, which is its wallet. They are poor revolutionaries who want to fix the attention of the proletarians on distant questions wreathed in ideological smoke. To renounce the struggle because "it's not worth the effort" is often the expression of a more generalized passivity.

Are we to fall into the trap of efficacy for efficacy's sake, into economism? No, but we do believe that class action tends to create its own content. That is why powers of every kind seek to suppress it.

Supporters of the most immediate and most varied possible forms of pressure and reaction on the part of the working class, we distrust many of the reform-oriented goals that are dissociated from immediate possibilities and relations of force. Even, and above all, when this involves a transitional program with a Trotskyist flavour. These performances, which allegedly have the goal of unifying and clarifying the proletariat, merely obscure the picture.

If it is true that it is right to struggle, and to struggle in the most generalized possible ways, in order to reduce working time, it is also true that it is hardly beneficial to set goals concerning the length of the working week or on the retirement age. This would merely be to accept them at face value and to internalize capitalist limitations and separations. The choice is between working time and free time, the condition of a convict or that of an inmate in a nursing home. The struggle is channelled and latent communism is sterilized.

The only acceptable perspective is communism. It is not a distant abstraction but the human solution for all problems. It involves the making manifest of the meaning of the proletarian movement, of showing the power that it possesses.

It is often the case that wars are not declared: absenteeism, interfering with the speed of the assembly line, sabotage, theft ... are the most effective. We do not turn them into fetishes. Capital can tolerate them and turn them into pressure valves. They cannot replace a more generalized struggle — but they do sustain fighting morale, they develop initiative and provide healthy and immediate satisfactions.

We have to popularize the means of action that, by putting immediate pressure on the exploiters, announce the communist world. It is often possible, in a hidden way but also massively and openly, to freely distribute products and perform services for free. The postal workers might deliver mail without stamps, the railroad conductors might not collect tickets. If the most militant workers are fired it will be necessary to reintegrate them in the struggle, by employing sabotage if necessary.

Our strategy can be expressed as: less useless talk, less spectacle, but the working class will use the countless means that it has at its disposal in order to make itself respected and to prepare the future. A little less of the spirit of serious reformism and a little more provocative and joyful laughter.

On the historical scale, the communist revolution is imminent. We are not writing for future generations.

By saying this, we know full well that many revolutionaries have already proclaimed the imminence of the revolution and were deceived. They regularly underestimated the system's capacities for adaptation. It seems that today, however, the shoe is on the other foot. Is it not the case that the capital's most recent bogus public image, that of its power and of its immortality, has been implanted in everyone's minds?

Machine technology having developed to the point of automation, it tends to unify the planet; it is at the peak of its power but it has also encountered its historical limits. It has no more answers for the destruction of the social fabric or for the degradation of the natural environment that it engenders. It cannot trim its own fat. It is its own power, its own concentration, that is rendering it powerless.

The crisis of economic civilization has gradually taken shape as an economic crisis. Poetic justice! But the current phase cannot be reduced to a temporary period of economic difficulties.

To escape from its crisis it is necessary to increase the rate of surplus value, and to restore the depressed profitability of capital. Many technical, ecological and human obstacles stand in the way of this goal. They can only be overcome by enormous struggles and changes. The proletariat is now showing, in a thousand ways, that it will not let history pass it by without its involvement. It is also showing that it will not settle for a reformist solution. A solution that would merely consist in assuring the proletariat's complicity in its own defeat and burial that would be worse than the defeat inflicted upon it by Stalinism and fascism.

9. Becoming Human

Communism is not a prisoner of the future. It arises from within capitalism. The actions carried out by the proletarians, when they spontaneously and usually unconsciously negate their own condition, is communist.

Communism presents itself in the first place, both as theory as well as practice, as an anticipation. From its origin, it looks like a solution for the evils of the old world, a solution that is more or less immediately feasible. Utopia is not just trash to be thrown away. It is, to the contrary, the characteristic sign of communism. We are more confident of the science of the future than in the present. But the future gnaws at the present.

Communism is certainly a stage of human history, a new world. But it is, above all, not just another social form but a privileged movement of the humanization of the species.

History

On the theoretical plane, communism appears with the renewal of ideas of the renaissance. In 1516, the Englishman Thomas More published his *Utopia* in Leuven. In 1602 the Dominican Campanella wrote his *City of the Sun*. He was in prison for having participated in an anti-Spanish conspiracy in Calabria. His book depicts a world in which money, property and class divisions do not exist, a world that he presents as an alternative to the present world. More, Campanella and others, who inclined towards communism, were not proletarians or even rebels. They were, rather, brilliant spiritual pioneers who flirted with the powers that be or who were persecuted due to their independence or their non-conformism.

During the same period, the times of the peasant war and Thomas Müntzer, communism began to take shape. It terrorized the princes, the bourgeoisie and the religious reformers, like Luther, who exclaimed: *"Unfortunate madmen! It is the voice of flesh and blood that got into your heads"*.

"They confuse faith with hope: is it not unnatural to believe, when nothing is possible?" "But what is serious is that the blessed hope that inspires them is not expected to be realized in another world, after death, but even on this earth, and as soon as possible."

– A Revolução dos Santos [The Revolution of the Saints 1520-1536], G. D'Aubarède, 1946

"But with regard to the Anabaptists of that era, we are hardly talking of religion at all. Their doctrine undermines the foundations of all social order, property, laws, magistrates...."

As for individual homes, each person accommodates himself as he pleases. Someone who previously slept out in the fields, sleeps in a hotel. The servants of the nobles and the clergy take over, without second thoughts, what had belonged to their lords.

"They burned the bishop's palace, the archives, the title deeds, the royal grants, all the documents. What possible use could such trivialities have for the New Zion, whose foundations were religious freedom and fraternal equality?"

– Jean Bockelson, M. Baston 1824

"Many people are unaware of the fact that communism had already become a practical fact in the domain of history, that it has provided its proofs, that it triumphed for several years and that it was violently affirmed in some provinces, no more than three hundred years ago.

"There were the same pretexts as today, more or less the same tendencies, the application of the same methods of action, but with powerful assistance, an avalanche of an immense force: the religious and mystical form that was assumed by the revolutionary powers of that epoch"

– Études historiques sur le communisme et les insurrections au XVIe siècle[/i] [Historical Studies on Communism and Insurrections in the 16th Century], Albert Arnoul, 1850

There are traces of the tendency to communism further back in time, even before the development of capitalism. It is the old aspiration to rediscover abundance and lost community.

The first practical attempts of modern communism were based on the remnants of primitive communism that had survived the development of class society.

Modern communism draws its inspiration from the old supporters of the community of goods: Plato, who advocated an aristocratic form of the community of goods for the members of the ruling class; and the early Christians, who shared their goods in common in accordance with the spirit of the Gospels.

Nonetheless, just as it is inspired by and connected to the past, modern communism also innovates.

Communism affirms itself as the enemy of the prevailing society, and attempts to replace it. Thomas More devoted the first part of his book to denouncing the evils of the present and discovering their causes. He demonstrated the harm caused by the development of capital.

Communism is no longer a state of mind nor a way of sharing resources in a life in common. It is a global and social solution, a way of organizing production.

Thomas More introduced a navigator, Hythloday, who visited the imaginary island of Utopia. Hythloday addressed the question of our society:

"Thoughtospeakplainlymyrealsentiments,"[/i] he said, "*I must freely own that as long as there is any property, and while money is the standard of all other things, I cannot think that a nation can be governed either justly or happily.... When, I say, I balance all these things in my thoughts, I grow more favourable to Plato, and do not wonder that he resolved not to make any laws for such as would not submit to a community of all things: for so wise a man could not but foresee that the setting all upon a level was the only way to make a nation happy, which cannot be obtained so long as there is property.... I am persuaded, that till property is taken away there can be no equitable or just distribution of things, nor can the world be happily governed....*"

More denounced the harm caused by the development of landed property and of agrarian capitalism which expelled the peasants from their land in order to replace them with sheep: [i]"... *your sheep, which are naturally mild, and easily*

kept in order, may be said now to devour men...."
He denounced the impotence of politics and the
distance that necessarily separates good precepts
from their practical application.

In Utopia things are different:

"Every city is divided into four equal parts, and
in the middle of each there is a marketplace ... and
thither every father goes and takes whatsoever he
or his family stand in need of, without either paying
for it or leaving anything in exchange. There is no
reason for giving a denial to any person, since there
is such plenty of everything among them; and there
is no danger of a man's asking for more than he
needs; they have no inducements to do this, since
they are sure that they shall always be supplied. It is
the fear of want that makes any of the whole race of
animals either greedy or ravenous...."

"In all other places," he writes, "it is visible that
while people talk of a commonwealth, every man
only seeks his own wealth; but there, where no man
has any property, all men zealously pursue the
good of the public...."

"In Utopia, where every man has a right to

everything, they all know that if care is taken to keep the public stores full, no private man can want anything ... there is no unequal distribution, so that no man is poor, none in necessity; and though no man has anything, yet they are all rich....

"Is not that government both unjust and ungrateful, that is so prodigal of its favors to those that are called gentlemen, or goldsmiths, or such others who are idle, or live either by flattery, or by contriving the arts of vain pleasure; and on the other hand, takes no care of those of a meaner sort, such as ploughmen, colliers, and smiths, without whom it could not subsist? But after the public has reaped all the advantage of their service, and they come to be oppressed with age, sickness, and want, all their labors and the good they have done is forgotten; and all the recompense given them is that they are left to die in great misery".

More concludes his book as follows: "... *there are many things in the Commonwealth of Utopia that I rather wish, than hope, to see followed in our governments.*" And the word, Utopia, means, in our everyday language, an unrealizable dream. And nonetheless....

And nonetheless, little more than a century later

an extraordinary experience unfolded that was similar to More's dream. It is very rare for a social project to be realized so faithfully.

Communism among the Guarani

In the year that *Utopia* was published, the Spaniards invaded and began their conquest of Paraguay: the country of the Guarani Indians. The name Paraguay designated, in the beginning, the homeland of the Guarani, a larger territory than the current Paraguay, so that the events that we shall discuss below also affected areas beyond the borders of the modern Paraguay.

Under the aegis of the Jesuits, hundreds of thousands of Indians would live, cultivate the soil, mine and forge metals, build shipyards, and practice the arts, without the use of money, wage labour, or the modern concept of property. The Republic of the Guaranis would endure for a century and a half, and would decline with the expulsion of the Jesuits and with the attacks of the Spaniards and the Portuguese. This zone was the most industrially advanced zone in Latin America in its time. Its contemporaries would investigate and debate about the nature and the importance of this experience that would be an inspiration for

European socialism. Some saw it as a pioneer effort, others minimized it or reduced it to a suspicious action of the Jesuits. With the passage of time the experience was considered to be too Jesuitical or too communist to merit attention.

The documents cited by the Papist Stalinophile, Clovis Lugon, allow us to form a more correct opinion (*La République des Guaranis*, Éditions Ouvrières, 1970).

"Nothing seems more beautiful to me than the order and the mode of providing for the needs of all the inhabitants of the colony. Those who reap the harvest are obliged to transport all their grain to public warehouses; there, people designated to guard these warehouses maintain a register of all that is received. At the beginning of every month, the people responsible for the administration of the granaries deliver to the regional supervisor the amount of grain that is needed by all the families of their zone, giving more or less to each family depending on how many mouths it has to feed"

– R. P. Florentin, Voyage aux Indes orientales

Most of the work is done in common and the Indians do not seem to be tempted by private property. They never possess more than a horse or a few chickens. In order to create private property individual lots were distributed, but on the day that the Indians were supposed to occupy these parcels they stayed home, *"stretched out in their hammocks..."* (P. Sepp).

"Father Cardiel, who deplored, so they said, the persistence of the communist system, did everything possible on his part to lead the Guaranis to private property and, above all, to a sense of individual interest and wealth, encouraging them to cultivate on their parcels of land products that have value with a view to selling the surplus. He frankly confessed his failure and declared that he had not found, at most, more than three examples of individuals who provided, from their parcels, a little sugar or cotton to sell. And one of the three was a converted mulatto!" (Lugon). And Father Cardiel added: *"In the twenty-eight years that I lived among them as priest or comrade, I never found a single example among so many hundreds of Indians."*

All the Indians were obliged to engage in manual labour and only spent a limited time engaged in such work: one third or one-half of the day.

"Everywhere, there are workshops of tinsmiths, painters, sculptors, goldsmiths, watchmakers, metal

workers, carpenters, cabinet makers, weavers, smelters—in a word, of all the arts and trades that people find useful" (Charlevoix). "Only in a great city in Europe would we find so many master artisans and artists" (Garech). "They make clocks, draft architectural plans, engrave geographical maps" (Sepp). According to Charlevois, the Guaranis "are instinctively gifted in all the arts to which they apply themselves.... They make the most complex organs after having seen one only once, and do the same with astronomical globes, Turkish-style carpets and everything that is most difficult to manufacture." And "as soon as the children reach the age when they can begin to work, they are led to the workshops and established in the one that seems to be most suited to their inclinations, because they are persuaded that art must be guided by nature."

The Indians also manufacture bells, firearms, cannons and munitions. Printing presses allow them to print books in many languages, mostly Guarani. The Indians were organized in military units; "they can immediately mobilize more than thirty thousand Indians, all on horseback" and are capable "of handling both muskets as well as sabres... of fighting in offensive as well as defensive formation, just like the Europeans." (Sepp). Father d'Aguilar, the Jesuit Superior General of the Republic, wrote: "We can *raise twenty thousand Indians who can hold their own against the best Spanish and Portuguese troops, against whom even the Mamelukes would not dare to fight, and who twice drove the Portuguese from the colony of Santo Sacramento, and who after so many years are respected by all the infidel nations that surround them."* (Quoted by Charlevoix).

Charlevoix continues: *"They only use gold and money to decorate their altars."* The population *obtains goods without money and without any kind of coinage."* Those idols of greed, Muratori says, are completely unknown to them…. The value of commodities is expressed in *"pesos"* and *"reals"* in a purely fictitious way. It was a way of establishing the relative value of everyday goods…. Alongside barter and fictitious money denominated in pesos, there is a *"real"* kind of coinage constituted by certain commodities in general use that were handled by every person as payment, even without having any need or immediate use for them … (tea, tobacco, honey, corn)….

"The price of goods normally corresponded to the real value of the goods or to the sum of labour required for their production, without added surcharges for the benefit of non-existent intermediaries. The relative price of a particular commodity was naturally influenced by its rarity or its abundance." (Lugon).

Trade between "reductions" depended on the communities. "The statistics regularly indicated the volume of reserves and the needs of each reduction and it was therefore easy to plan trade. The Father met with the magistrate and with the steward in order to determine the kind and the amount of commodities to import and to export." (Lugon).

Was this real communism?

Guarani communism was not pure communism. It was instilled with pious spirit of the Jesuits, it paid taxes to the King of Spain and provided military forces from the Guarani troops, it still had exchange relations, etc. But we are not looking for purity.

Nor were the Jesuits, who led the communism of the Guaranis, communists. They found themselves in the land of the Guaranis and they had to accommodate themselves to it. Some people rejoiced, finding the communism of the Guaranis be in conformance with the spirit of the Gospels, while others, due to their own inclinations or due to outside pressure, sought to undermine it. The Jesuits allowed the introduction of western technologies and knowledge into an ineradicable primitive communism. They allowed the Guarani groups to unite into an impressive whole.

This communism was sufficiently communist to

provoke mistrust and attacks. The Jesuits played a rather nefarious role, since they were subject to an authority that was external to the Guarani community, sowing confusion and disunity as soon as the Spaniards and the Portuguese attacked the eastern "reductions" in 1754-1756. *"The Fathers of the reductions had received from the Superior General of the Company, Ignacio Visconti, 'strict orders to submit to the inevitable and lead the Indians to obedience'."* (Lugon). The Indians who were directly threatened fought back, but were finally crushed. In 1768 the Jesuits were expelled. The anti-Guarani expeditions continued and destroyed the communist project. The weakness of Guarani communism was the fact that, from the very beginning, it was not a revolutionary communism and it was not constituted in a confrontation.

In 1852, Martin de Moussy wrote: *"the best proof that this strange regime, this communism that was so severely criticized perhaps with a semblance of reason, was suited to the Indians, is that the successors of the Jesuits were forced to allow it to continue to exist right up until recently and that its destruction, not prepared with intelligent and paternalistic measures, had no other result than that of plunging the Indians into poverty ... today, their heirs bitterly regret the absence of that regime, undoubtedly an imperfect one, but one that was very well adapted to their instincts and their customs."*

Lugon, who sought to impute to the Jesuits the role of importers of communism, also wrote:

"Soon after the destruction of Entre-Rios, the survivors reorganized under the direction of three chiefs assisted by a council, precisely following the traditions bequeathed by the Jesuits. The population of this colony was estimated at 10,000 people between 1820 and 1827. The community of goods was therefore integrally restored.

"In the reductions attributed to modern Paraguay, the communist regime was officially abolished in 1848 by the dictator Lopez. The Guaranis who continued to live in this region were, at that time, legally dispossessed of their homes and their possessions. They were left to vegetate in reservations organized in the North American style."

The Republic of the Guaranis is not the only example of an encounter between Indian communism and the west. There have been some others of lesser importance: the Chiquito Republic in southwestern Bolivia, the Republic of the Moxos in northern Bolivia, the group of the Pampas....

The communists of Munzer or of Paraguay lasted longer than the Communards (of Paris) and other proletarians of modern times and created an intermediate social form between primitive communism and higher communism. Would they have regressed with the passage of time? It was the power of capital and the degradation that this power causes to the social meaning of individuals that stood against communism. It would not have regressed but rather undergone a cycle that returns to its origins and that would only see communism reborn but this time in the heart of the capitalist world.

This is perhaps incomprehensible for those who see history as a linear and continuous process. Where there is no regression, there is no anticipation, but rather a perpetual progress from the lower to the higher. Why, then, did modern industry emerge from European feudal backwardness rather than from the great cloth manufacturing centres of the Incas, or from Chinese art and technology? Why was that industry only capable of being introduced after a period of decline?

Familiar with and in the wake of this communism with a religious disguise, although it was iconoclastic in the case of the German insurrectionaries or Campanella who wanted to put an end to the family, a naturalist and anti-religious communism developed in the wake of the bourgeois revolutions.

The Levellers

In England, after the revolution of 1648, a pro-communist current developed within the party of the "Levellers". Many communist works appeared during this period. These texts advocated the obligation for all to work and the free distribution of goods.

Contacts with non-western societies nourished philosophical reflections. In 1704, Nicolas Gueudeville published the *Conference or Dialogue between the Author [the Baron de Lahontan] and Adario, a Noted Man among the Savages*. The Indian is superior to the European because he does not know the distinction between *"mine"* and *"thine"*.

In 1755, Morelly published his *Code of Nature*. In this book he affirmed that man was neither bad nor vicious. He has to break with *"the desire for possessions"* and with property.

"If you were to take away property, the

blind and pitiless self-interest that accompanies it, you would cause all the prejudices in errors that they sustain to collapse. There would be no more resistance, either offensive or defensive, among men; there would be no more furious passions, ferocious actions, notions or ideas of moral evil."

Despite his faith in human nature, Morelly proceeded, contradictorily, to define the laws that should rule the life of people to its smallest details. Clothing, houses, divorce, the education of children, thoughts and even dreams are strictly regulated.

Morelly's communism would particularly influence the revolutionary Gracchus Babeuf who would be executed in 1797 after the failure of the Conspiracy of the Equals.

It was basically correct to consider that communism corresponds to human nature, that it is the natural condition of the species. This is not because man is spontaneously good or moral, nor is it because societies succeed one another without modifying an unalterable human nature. It is simply because classes, property, exchange, and the state are imposed as social, and therefore human, necessities, but do not pass from being momentary necessities that correspond to the passage from one communist social form to another. Communism is not imposed. It constantly arises even if it can only develop at certain moments. We see that a spontaneous and typically human manifestation like speech is communist, at least at a formal level. With respect to its own understanding, communism is much simpler, much more transparent than capitalism: the dominant social form. This is because it is, even today, a more immediate reality. When we ridicule the rich bourgeoisie because of his express monopoly on money and when we seem to be naïve, this is because we can directly rely upon a communist conception of wealth that exists in a latent state.

We are accused of being simple minded or naïve. Up to a certain point, these are virtues that we cultivate. Blessed are the poor in spirit, for theirs is the kingdom of heaven; and not just that. Communism is not accused of being incomprehensible and unacceptable but rather of being naïve, for not taking account of the reality that it seeks to overthrow. But communism is fought because it is known that it is not so naïve and that the means for its success exist.

Theory is necessary. It is necessary in a world in which human reality escapes the control of humans. But if theory only serves to complicate matters, to reinforce the veil that separates men from their humanity, then it would be better to abstain from it. Revolutionary theory is not like the theory of relativity. It addresses a reality within which we are immersed. The complexity and the separation that it seeks to reduce, in the movement that, for that very reason, is properly communist, is not linked to physical reasons but to human reasons that can be changed by humans.

It is tempting to either remain addicted to theory and thus to reject life or to reject theory and to drug ourselves with life. In the absence of life, the separation of the mechanisms that organize the life of man does not lead to an active will to forcibly understand but is actually an unbridled quest for images, for possibilities of identification. What matters is not to understand and thus to enter into the possibility of transforming reality but finding responsible elements, culprits, warmongers and thieves of labour. It is merely due to this quest for the concrete and for images that the system and its managers have succeeded in concentrating the people's hatred against this or that social group. Against this perverted need for life we must oppose explanation but above all life itself. Drug addicts cannot be cured with words.

Morelly says: *"It is unfortunately all too true that to form a republic of this sort would be just about impossible at the present time."* The utopians did not grasp the movement that could lead to communism. In that epoch, the proletariat still seemed to be too weak as an autonomous social force. But the utopian descriptions already manifested the historical necessity of communism and transformed it into an immediate demand in conformity with its profound nature.

The future is not a point that is outside the reality in which we live. It is this reality, it is its supersession. Communism is, here and elsewhere, today and tomorrow, my subjectivity and the objective development of the forces of production. We cannot, without deceiving ourselves, oppose communism as utopia to communism as historical movement. One of the great merits of the utopians was the fact that they did not nourish any illusions concerning the historical possibilities of their proposals.

It was only later that we see communist reformers like Cabet and Owen who tried to cause their ideas to become reality by way of the creation of small communities or "communist" or communist-inspired institutions.

The strength of utopianism is that it did not waste time constructing a representation of the developmental process leading to utopia, to deduce what will be from what is. It directly anticipates utopia. It works radically, that is, at the human level, with the problems that capital poses and directly imposes. Problems that humanity will be forced to solve some day.

As utopia, communism affirms itself in its discontinuity with the present. It is conceived as a new global equilibrium.

This concept of communism is opposed by a vulgar determinism that reduces development to a continuous process in which each phase is the extension or the copied product of the preceding phase. The utopian is reduced to a dreamer or a mystical rationalist. It is not perceived that his attitude is not his starting point but a part of the movement in question.

Communism is the expression of the unfolding, historically permitted and ordered, of the capacities of the human species. It is the natural condition of the species. But this nature is historically produced. History is merely limited to ordering and masticating over and over again the same materials without, however, coming to a halt or describing a closed circle.

The intermediate phase of class societies, which tends to negate man by transforming him into an instrument, does not make communism possible and necessary except due to the characteristics that are inherent to and genetically inscribed within the species. It was the human capacity for adaptation and also for submission, to use but also to be used as an instrument, that was turned against humanity. This phase, by engendering capitalism and machinery, signed its own death sentence.

Scientific Socialism

In the 19th century, the antagonism between the bourgeoisie and the proletariat became the predominant antagonism. Communism began to be less of a demand of reason or of philosophy in general. It sought to inscribe itself in and to become the practice of reality. The first tendency that arose was the one that sought to begin to create islands of communism and to propagate communism by example, gradually and with the agreement of the powerful. The second tendency that arose was that of revolutionary and insurrectionary communism. In France, this tendency is mainly associated with the name of Blanqui:

"Communism, which is revolution itself, must distrust the allure of utopia and must never separate from politics. Up until recently it was on the outside. Today, it is in our hearts. It is only our servant. It should not be overworked, however, if we want to retain its services. It cannot be imposed suddenly, either immediately or the day after the victory. You might as well try to reach the sun. Before we got very high, we would end up on the ground with broken limbs a nice trip to the hospital."

Blanqui already saw communism in action— still, in our opinion, in a somewhat exaggerated way—in the capitalist world:

"Taxes, and government itself, are communism, certainly of the worst kind, but nonetheless absolutely necessary.... Association, in the service of capital, is becoming a curse that will not be endured for much longer. It is the privilege of this glorious principle that it can only work for the good."

– 'Le Communisme, avenir de la société' [Communism, the Future of Society], 1869

Communism, by being openly linked with the struggle of the proletariat, took a decisive step forward but was also perverted. It allowed itself to gradually cease to be an immediate demand. It became a project, a mission, a historical stage separate from the present. Emptied of its content by the "levellers" and the "compartmentalizers" it would be transformed, in the twentieth century into a disguise for capital.

"Scientific socialism" was one way to rationalize the historical postponement of communism. In the 19th century, the working class was still capable of autonomous action but communism was not possible. By proposing political methods and transitional stages, Bray, Marx and Blanqui opened the door to all kinds of recuperations.

It is precisely communism that is lacking in the celebrated *Communist Manifesto*. In that work we find an apology for the bourgeoisie, an analysis of class struggles, and transitional measures. Of communism, it says little and what it does say is bad.

The Manifesto was drafted for the "League of the Just", which became the "Communist League". Before Marx and Engels joined this group, the doctrine of this association of immigrant German artisans and workers was somewhat confused. Weitling, its founder and theoretician, was a mystical type. Marx and Engels succeeded in bringing indisputable progress but also provoked regression with respect to an ingenuous but more positive and even more correct affirmation of communism.

In June of 1847 the Congress of the League of the Just proclaimed its objectives in Article 1 of its Statutes: *"The League has the goal of suppressing the slavery of men by the dissemination of the theory of the community of goods and its practical application as soon as possible."*

In November 1846/February 1847, the Central Committee had written to the Sections: *"You know that communism is a system according to which the Earth must be the common property of all men, according to which all persons must work, 'produce', according to their abilities and enjoy, 'consume', according to their efforts...."*

Article I of the new Statutes, written by Marx and Engels, emphasized the problems of power and domination and defined communism negatively: *"The aim of the league is the overthrow of the bourgeoisie, the rule of the proletariat, the abolition of the old bourgeois society which rests on the antagonism of classes, and the foundation of a new society without classes and without private property."*

In *Der Hilferuf der deutschen Jugend* [The Cry for Help of German Youth] (1841), Weitling defined his Christian communism as follows:

"The problem that he [Christ] posed was the founding of a kingdom on the whole earth, freedom for all nations, the community of goods and labor for all who profess the kingdom of God. And it is precisely this that the communists of today once again adopt...."

"There are communists who are communists without knowing it: the hard working farmer who shares his piece of black bread with the hungry worker is a communist, the hard working artisan who does not exploit his workers and who pays them in proportion to the product of their common labor is a communist, the rich man who spends his extra money for the good of suffering humanity is a communist...."

Communism and charity are practically confounded. Marx correctly and vigorously reacted against this confusion. But in the *Communist Manifesto* the communists are not any more well defined by their communism. They are simply the most resolute of the proletarians and the ones who have the advantage of a clear awareness of the line of advance of the proletarian movement: the possessors of theory.

At the end of the 19th and beginning of the 20th century, and this despite the anger Marx displayed against the Social Democracy, primarily against the Gotha Congress of 1875, communism was emptied of its real content. It only retained its profound meaning among a small handful of anarchists.

In 1891, Paul Reclus, to justify *"individual expropriation"*, that is, theft, offered the following brief and good definition of communism in *La Revolte*:

"Activity, in life as we imagine it might be, is so unlike the one we lead now that what we call work, we shall call theft: to take something without asking and this is not theft; to offer something from our own abilities and activity and this will not be work."

With the revolutionary wave that followed the First World War and in the outbreak of the Russian Revolution, Marxist and communist tendencies re-emerged. There are vestiges of the memory of communism in the Bolsheviks. These vestiges would quickly be perverted and would disappear with the defeat of the world revolution and in the swamp of Russian problems.

It was right to denounce the extremely precocious counterrevolutionary role of the Bolsheviks, as it was also correct to demonstrate the bourgeois character of Lenin's theoretical and practical work. But it is stupid to want to hold the Bolsheviks responsible for the failure of the workers' revolution in Russia. The Bolsheviks were, above all, a specific case of an example of a handful of men who managed to change the course of history as far as revolutionary possibilities would allow. Their adversaries, even those to their left, generally only used humanist and democratic perspective to oppose them.

The contrast between the importance of the revolutionary wave and the failure of the communist affirmation is impressive.

In Germany and Holland it was mainly "the left" that denounced the Russian regime as state capitalism. Against Russian state capitalism, they opposed a communism based on workers' management. We must grant that they highlighted the autonomous action of the masses and of the workers' councils. With the defeat of the revolution, this current, represented above all by the KAPD, fragmented into tiny sects, after having organized hundreds of thousands of workers.

This ideology of workers' self-management would also be used by the anarchists and by the anarcho-syndicalists. Communism is reduced to the self-organization of the producers.

It was in Italy that the left fraction of Bordiga, who was a dominant figure in the founding of the PCI, made the most effective contribution to the restoration of communist doctrine. He took a position against participation in elections, he repudiated united fronts with social democracy, he criticized the democratic illusion. He emphasized the abolition of wage labour and of the commodity economy. Bordiga, mostly after the Second World War, developed his analysis of the capitalist counterrevolution in Russia and his conception of communism. Communism is not built; commodity society is destroyed.

Despite its profound contributions, Bordigism did not succeed in freeing itself from its Leninist ambiance. Its radicalism and its perspicacity became mired in the worst dead ends.

After the Second World War, theoretical communism was only very gradually reborn. The prosperity and good health of capital did not help it. After having been ground to a pulp, with only a few remnants remaining, it had to overcome its past. It developed as the social crisis—and then the economic crisis—of capital once again became visible.

After having rediscovered the critique of the Eastern Bloc and the bureaucracy, the Situationists elaborated a theory of modern society based on the commodity and the "spectacle". They denounced modern misery. However pertinent their analyses often might have appeared to be, they still remained on the surface of things. They were still prisoners, with regard to both their style and their content, of the spectacle effect that they denounced and reflected.

The Situationists produced a brilliant and corrosive social critique, but not a theory of capital, of the machinery that upholds the spectacle, or of the revolution. They did not address the question of communization by praising the immediate negation of the commodity (looting and arson) or by immersing themselves in councilism (the absolute power of the workers' councils upon which everything depends). They were fierce enemies of Bolshevism, but like the Bolsheviks they made the revolution a question of organization.

The communist doctrine must focus on the description of the future and above all on the process of communization. It is in this respect that it must be discussed, that unites or separates. It is not a matter of fleeing the present but of living and of judging in the light of the future. Communism is here and now and its perspectives can be immediately opposed to the capitalist view.

Struggles, if they do not lead to positive perspectives, thus showing their lack of depth, become just another means of wallowing in misery on the pretext of denunciation. Like clowns and comedians, ideologists end up feeding on the decomposition of the system. If we can forgive everyone who makes us laugh, these people can never be forgiven. The ultimate form of concealing the gigantic and unexplored possibilities that are open to humanity: the ultimate form of extinguishing hope in the hearts of the oppressed!

With the passage of time, the communist idea and struggle re-emerge constantly. Nonetheless, they are only transformed to the extent that, as they are recuperated, capitalism is forced to overcome them. Today, since capitalism generalizes public property and concentrated labour, communism goes beyond the opposition between individual and collective appropriation. It is no longer based on the question of property. Communism no longer oscillates between an asocial naturalism and a moralism or an exasperated regulationism.

The Marxist stage must not be spared, either. Communism was considered to be a mode of production that would succeed capitalism. It is at the same time more than that and something beyond a social form. It is the movement, in the heart of capitalism, which rejects it, by which human activity breaks its chains and finally flourishes!

Communist Activity

Communism is, first, activity. First, because it

arises from within capitalism before it can overthrow capitalism. First, because in the communist world human activity and its vital functions are not the prisoners of previously produced social forms. The organization of tasks does not have to be crystallized in institutions.

Communism erupts positively from within capitalism. But it affirms itself as the other side of negation. Communism as activity is at the same time negation and anticipation: there will not be two successive moments. The more activity is turned against capital the more it will tend to present an outline of communism and vice-versa.

It is therefore not a matter, by any means, of building islands of communism within capitalism. If activity tends towards construction it will destroy the communist point of view.

There will not be communist needs that will demand their satisfaction beyond the system. Just as there will be needs in communism, when they arise they cannot be dissociated from their possibilities of realization, even imaginary, in the system. The inability of capitalism to satisfy desires leads to its abolition and to the abolition of the desires that it permits.

We do not see communism as Weitling did in the moral sense or as Blanqui did in the rise of the glorious principle of association. If that is communism, it is negative communism, and not to be confused with bad communism. It is the ascent of the movement of capitalist robbery.

Dispossessed of the instruments of production, deprived of the power over their labour, separated from each other but confronting and operating an enormous productive power, gathered together in great masses, the proletarians see communism inscribed negatively in their situation. They do not have, any more than they possess their own means of production, particular interests to defend. Their dispossession confronts the power and the social wealth that they create. And it is this that makes the proletariat the class of communism. The proletarians cannot re-appropriate, a little at a time, the means of production. They have to take them in common.

But what is fundamental is not so much—just as things are indissociably connected—the movement of re-appropriation and possessing goods in common, but the new activity that unfolds, the re-appropriation of life, the birth of new relations, the destruction of the relation of domination between men and objects.

It is true that communism, the human community, is a stage of historical development. The antagonisms that oppose human groups and interests will disappear.

But one cannot understand communism if it is established as a goal or as a completed movement, separate from the activity that produces it. By subordinating activity to the goal, the means to the ends, one only projects into history the rule of capital-commodity over human activity, which it imprisons in the labour form. The end, the result, communist social forms, must be considered a necessity of activity that seeks to assure and to reproduce its conditions of existence.

Community is in the future society, in the unification of the planet, in the end of the division of the economy into enterprises, a global and social solution. But those who do not see the spontaneous activity of the proletarians in action, who do not see the immediate and individual negation of racism and lies, understand nothing.

The relation between immediate activity and the future world is crucial. The universality of communism is contained in the particularity of situations.

If this universality can erupt from the particular it is through that particular being, itself the product of the universal, unifying and private logic of capital.

Those who do not perceive the connection are obliged to appeal to a false universal: the party (proletarian!), the state (proletarian!) or even the proletariat as an abstraction or representation. This false universal is itself considered as containing the active principle as against an inert social mass. The instrument and its object. The spirit transforming or riding matter.

Communist consciousness is only generalized when society is shaken to its foundations. But in resurgent life all of this is already there, including the consciousness that ceases to be the passive reflection of congealed representations and situations. Ideological consciousness is transformed into practical consciousness. This is already communist.

The more intense the struggle becomes, the more do those who participate in it discover that they are liberated from the prejudices and pettiness to which they had become accustomed. Their consciousness is shaken to its roots and they look at reality and the existence that they had led in a new and shocking way.

This presence of communism is not the monopoly of the struggle in the strict sense of the word: an open and declared battle between labour and capital. It is manifested throughout all of social life and often abandons those ritualized, fossilized and tedious struggles which are no longer really struggles.

The true human community always implies a contradiction with capital. It tends to become an open struggle or is destroyed and recuperated to become an image used to disguise reality. The growing influence of capital over life increasingly expels and renders impossible all real humanity, all love, all creation and exploration. Men are being turned into empty carcases that walk without life to the rhythms of capital. Revolt and reaction must therefore obtain a more and more human character. This humanity that contradicts capital, the necessary stage of the becoming of the species, is what we call communism. This label is still necessary insofar as this human future cannot claim to represent or encompass all human manifestations because it remains antagonistic to capital.

Communism is possible because capital cannot transform men into robots. Even if it robotizes their existence it cannot do without their humanity. The most integrated and most servile activity feeds on participation, creation, communication and initiative despite the fact that these qualities cannot possibly develop fully and freely. Necessity and earning a salary are not enough to make the worker functional. This requires other motivations, it requires his contribution. The labour-form cannot function without the generic, human character of the worker's activity.

We saw (in Chapter IV) that the separate spheres of life are only perpetuated and maintained in their unity: it is impossible to completely dissociate production, education and experimentation. Even the least intelligent production or labour demands a certain adaptation of the worker and the ability to confront unexpected situations. In the same way, the most abstract education must be concretized by way of certain "products", which are not made by copying an exam. The needs of control from the outside fall upon production....

The system of production would collapse if the workers were to cease to experiment, to help each other and to hold discussions. The hierarchical organization of labour can only survive if its rules are permanently ignored. It imposes an unenforceable framework on the infractions and the spontaneous activity of the workers in order to prevent them from undergoing further development and from becoming really dangerous and subversive. When a breach opens up or a conflict breaks out this activity tends to become autonomous and to develop according to its own logic.

By fighting, the proletariat immediately denies itself as wage labour, as slave, as robot. However limited the reappearance of life and of action, capitalist oppression is there if it challenges its foundations.

The proletarian who was nothing but a cog in the machinery starts to learn again, to strive, to take risks. He rediscovers control over his deeds. His eyes open, his intelligence stirs. The oppressive spirit of seriousness, the tedium that shackles men in the galleys of Wage Labour and the policed and commodified world, are overthrown. Everything becomes possible.

The revolt as a search for pleasure and efficacy finds itself beyond labour. His wage is found directly in the happiness that he awakens and its results.

The wildcat activity of the proletariat is repressed when it goes beyond a certain limit. More currently, it is recuperated and directed into a stillborn state. Thus, it is not just communism, it is the product of capitalism as capitalism is the product of communism. If we insist upon this latent or inchoate communism it is not in order to idolize it. It can only be itself by going beyond and exiting the capitalist orbit. To recognize its importance is not same as bowing down before a spontaneity that refuses to organize itself, discipline itself and take the offensive.

Capital recuperates in conformity with its

profound nature. It is essentially a vampire. It is therefore necessary for us not to allow ourselves to be dazzled by this or that spectacular aspect of it.

The workers' struggles, despite the opposition that they trigger, help the system to change and realize its potential, while it always remains itself. Wage and political struggles, or wage and political solutions, shake the system up and allow it to modernize itself.

The incipient struggle is sterilized at the root. The strike, the demonstration, the occupation of the factory tend to conform to a well-worn channel. They do not seek to harm capital but to treat its illness, to express discontent. In increasing alienation the strike does not appear as a means of pressure but as a sacrifice for those who engage in it. This is demonstrated by the importance of sacrifice to the gravity of the protest. The social war is replaced by the parade.

Activity and Program

The point of view of activity is that of communism. It is not a matter of denying the need for activity to materialize, but of objectivizing it and of supporting whatever it engenders and transforms.

Capital, to the contrary, only considers activity

from the point of view of the thing produced. It is by that means that it assimilates, as a foreign force, labour and specifically human activity. Activity is only seriously carried out with a view to its immediate and positive contribution. Positive according to capital.

This will to only consider the immediate impact conceals the character of anticipation of the workers' struggle:

"Instead of looking at what the workers do, the bourgeois ideologues try to imagine what the workers want to obtain. They do not see proletarian activity except as a factor of disturbance or modernization of the system, never as the outline of its abolition".

– "Lordstown 72 ou Les déboires de la General Motors", Les amis de 4 millions de jeunes travailleurs, 1977

This activity is not seriously carried out because it is not productive. It would be purely destructive or negative. How could one think that it could inspire a new world? In reality, the negative character of communist activity is determined by the immediate de 4 millions de jeunes travailleurs, 1977). Just as this destructive character eventually disappears when the worker produces on his own account at the cost of his enterprise.

By making proletarian activity the pivot of our doctrine we can perceive the identity and the discontinuity between revolt against capital and the future world. We see a contradictory unity of labour and communist activity. We can affirm that communism is, first of all, a radical transformation of human activity rather than a modification of the social forms. This allows us to re-evaluate the traditional ideas about the calculation of costs in the communist world.

In his youthful writings, Marx conceived communism not only as a movement but also as activity. Unfortunately, as he elaborated his conception of historical development, this point of view faded away as a unitary point of view. Marx became a communist theoretician of capitalism in both senses of the expression. On the one hand, he analysed capitalism from the point of view of its negation. On the other, he is the prisoner of capitalism.

Obviously, Marx took human activity into consideration as revolutionary activity and as productive activity, but separately. With regard to the Revolution of 1848, he shows that proletarian activity was nourished by its class situation and developed according to its own logic. In his economic works he made labour the basis of the measure of value. But by deducing productive activity from the product he fell back upon the assimilation between human productive activity and labour. He did not see the activity of the revolutionary proletariat as something "beyond labour".

If everything rests on the immediate activity of the proletariat, why do we have to occupy ourselves merely with theory, with organization? Why should we formulate a program?

Not everything is in the immediate activity of the proletariat, it is just that everything must be connected to it, that everything must be put into perspective and in resonance. Immediate activity is only communist by virtue of its capacity to go beyond itself.

The communist program is a necessity, even if it is momentarily separated from the proletariat as a whole. It is not outside of its movement but without an anticipation, a guide. Its truth resides in its ability to be dissolved, that is, realized by the class. It is merely the program of proletarian activity.

Index

C

Y

Z

un monde sans argent :
le communisme

« Ainsi
l'URSS n'est
pas communiste
mais les Etats-Unis
l'Amérique l'étaient
il y a encore
quelques siècles »
(p. 12)

1

LES AMIS DE 4 MILLIONS
DE JEUNES TRAVAILLEURS
B.P. 1604
75002 PARIS CEDEX 04

un monde sans argent :

le communisme

2

LES AMIS DE ... MAISON
DE JEUNES TRAVAILLEURS
B.P. ...
...

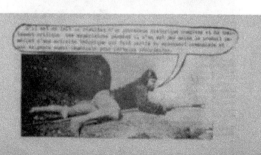

images of the first prints of A World Without
Money: Communism in French, zine format

Radical Reprints

The Radical Database

Linktree

A WORLD WITHOUT MONEY: COMMUNISM

BY THE FRIENDS OF 4 MILLION YOUNG WORKERS